The Experts' Guide
to 100 Things
Everyone Should Know
How to Do

The Experts' Guide to 100 Things Everyone Should Know How to Do

CREATED BY

SAMANTHA ETTUS

CLARKSON POTTER/PUBLISHERS

NEW YORK

CONTENTS

✳

WORK LIFE

✳

❋

WEEKEND LIFE

❋

*

THE BIG LIFE

*

INTRODUCTION

E VERY DAY we fake it a little bit. We use big words (but don't ask us to define them); we sew buttons (but don't look under the fabric); and we eat right (but don't peek in our fridge)!

Let's face it. Though we could (and often do) live our lives hiding what we don't know and flaunting what we do, if we learned the fundamentals of these everyday tasks, life would be better, wouldn't it? We would no longer have to cut the corners, talk around the issues, and fudge the numbers.

Over the years, I have accumulated a seemingly endless list—a black hole of skills I somehow never acquired on my way to adulthood. I call this my Personal Knowledge Gap. And while I assumed that wisdom would come with age, my Knowledge Gap doesn't seem to be getting smaller. In fact, now that I have three children, the list of things I don't know only seems to be growing as I discover how much more there is to learn. In sharing my list with friends, I realized I wasn't alone. My most "together" friend sheepishly admitted that she has no idea how to iron a shirt; another confessed that he is on an endless quest for the perfect shave.

With so many things to know, I realized that we all need the Cliff Notes to life, and I set out to create one. I limited my list to 100 questions, and I began the search for the right experts to answer them. Thus began *The Experts' Guide to 100 Things Everyone Should Know How to Do.*

Each contributor in this book has been painstakingly selected from among their distinguished peers as *the* expert on their subjects. Finding them was challenging but thoroughly fun. Though Howard Stephen Berg knows he is the fastest reader in the world, Cory Booker, a New Jersey Senator who gives more than 400 speeches a year, might never take credit for being one of the world's greatest orators. And while many of us turn to Suze Orman for money saving advice, we might not have realized that the key to snow shoveling resides in the mind of the Mayor of Buffalo.

My quest for small improvements became a game. When walking home from work one night in New York, I felt an icy chill and was hungry for some tips on how best to stay warm. But who to turn to? Jim Whittaker, the first American to climb Mount Everest, would definitely have the answer. When I realized my hospital corners were beyond lacking, I sought out advice from Tracey Henderson, the Holiday Inn Housekeeper of the Year to share the secret to flawlessly make a bed. Why should my family settle for runny eggs, when surely famed chef Jean Georges Vongerichten could teach me the best way to cook them? And what if my perfect eggs could be accompanied by a lesson in newspaper reading? Arthur Sulzberger, Jr., Publisher of *The New York Times,* gave me permission to skip some sections and Dr. Dean Ornish taught me to relax about it. Why settle for clutter when organizational expert Julie Morgenstern could teach me the tricks to saving space? When I was late to a post-work dinner with my family, I looked to business-management guru Stephen Covey for a lesson in time management.

As I thought about the litany of subjects that needed expertise, they naturally grouped themselves into categories that reflect the structure of our lives.

- MORNING LIFE, from washing your hair to driving to work
- WORK LIFE, from shaking hands to speaking in public
- HOME LIFE, from training a dog to picking produce
- WEEKEND LIFE, from washing a car to making a martini
- THE BIG LIFE, from flirting to planning a wedding

Even if you aren't ready to plan a wedding, you can always start with the more manageable events—a dinner party perhaps? In my case, this book has given me the confidence to finally throw one right. Andrew Firestone's advice ensures that I will never again serve cork with my wine, Peggy Post has finally eased my butter-knife anxiety, and Ira Glass has offered the inside tips on telling a great story while Larry King chimed in with the best way to listen to one.

So now it is time to invite you to be my guest on this journey. In this book I know you will discover new ways to do things better. But I also hope you find that you are already an expert in something. After identifying the 100 experts in this book and the three that have followed, I became comfortable counting talent-spotting among my own areas of expertise. So read on, polish your skills, and if I haven't spotted you yet, drop me a note.

MORNING
LIFE

SLEEP

JAMES B. MAAS

*

*James B. Maas, PhD, is a Stephen H. Weiss
Presidential Fellow, Professor, and
past Chairman of Psychology at Cornell University.
He is the recipient of the American Psychological
Association's Outstanding Educator Award and
the author of* Power Sleep.

TREATING sleep as a necessity rather than a luxury is the secret to being a peak performer. When you don't get proper sleep, you experience daytime drowsiness, increased stress, feelings of lethargy, mood shifts, weight gain, reduced immunity to disease and viral infection, and lowered productivity, concentration, and memory. Even modest sleep deprivation can seriously affect your general health and longevity!

How do you know if you are getting proper sleep? Answer the following questions:

- Do I need an alarm clock in order to wake up at the appropriate time?
- Do I often fall asleep in boring meetings or in warm rooms, after heavy meals, or when watching TV?
- Do I often fall asleep within 5 minutes of getting into bed?
- Do I often sleep extra hours on weekend mornings?
- Do I feel tired during the day?

If you answered yes to any of these questions, it's likely you need more sleep.

THE GOLDEN RULES OF SLEEP

1. GET PROPER SLEEP

Identify the amount of sleep you need to be fully alert all day long and get that amount every night. For most adults, it's 8 hours. For teenagers, it's 9.25 hours.

2. ESTABLISH A REGULAR SLEEP SCHEDULE

Go to bed at the same time every night, and wake up (without an alarm clock) at the same time every morning—including weekends.

3. GET CONTINUOUS SLEEP

For sleep to be rejuvenating, you should get your required amount of sleep in one continuous block. Any nicotine or caffeine after 2 P.M. or alcohol within 3 hours of bedtime will disrupt your sleep.

4. MAKE UP FOR LOST SLEEP

For every 2 hours awake, you add 1 hour of debt to your sleep debt bank account—that is, it takes 8 hours of sleep to restore 16 hours of waking activity. You cannot make up for large sleep losses during the week by sleeping in on weekends any more than you can make up for lack of regular exercise and overeating during the week by working out and dieting only on the weekends. To make up for lost sleep, you might consider a power nap: taken midday and limited to 20 minutes.

SLEEP STRATEGIES

1. KEEP YOUR BEDROOM QUIET, DARK, AND COOL

Sleep on a mattress with individual pocketed coils that reduce motion transfer, or a foam mattress designed to support your back properly. Use a high-quality down pillow.

2. REDUCE STRESS AS MUCH AS POSSIBLE

Even if you are sleep-deprived, anxiety can delay sleep onset. Try relaxation exercises. Have a "worry time" before going to sleep by writing down your concerns. Your worries then won't interfere with sleep onset or wake you up during the night. Don't watch TV or surf the Internet within 2 hours of bedtime. Take a warm bath before bed. Reading for pleasure before turning off the lights will also ease you into sleep.

The best predictor of quality of life is sleep.

MAKE A BED

TRACEY R. HENDERSON

*

*Tracey R. Henderson is the Holiday Inn
Executive Housekeeper of the Year 2003.
She is currently the Executive Housekeeper at
the Holiday Inn Select in Norfolk, VA.*

ITEMS needed:

1 mattress pad	1 blanket
1 fitted sheet	2 pillowcases
1 flat sheet	1 bedspread

First, spread out the mattress pad over the mattress, covering it from head to foot. Then take your fitted sheet and place it over the mattress pad so that your mattress pad is snug. Place the flat sheet on the bed wrong side up. Then do the same with the blanket. At the base of the bed, tuck in both the flat sheet and the blanket (start from the center and work your way to the corners). Now, take the loose end of the sheet on one side of the foot of the bed and pull it straight up onto the bed, forming a triangular fold (picture 1). Tuck the hanging end of the sheet under the mattress (picture 2). Pull the triangular fold over the mattress (picture 3) and tuck that in nice and neat. Complete this process on the other side of the bed.

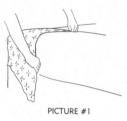

PICTURE #1

At the head of the bed, fold the blanket and flat sheet down 4 inches and tuck the sides in neatly. Now, put the bedspread on the bed, making sure there are equal amounts on all sides so that the spread doesn't touch the floor. Fold down about 3½ feet of the spread from the head of the bed.

PICTURE #2

It is now time to cover the pillows. In-

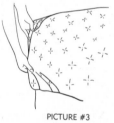

PICTURE #3

sert the pillows into the pillowcases. Fold the open end of both pillowcases inward so that the ends look finished. Place the pillows side by side on the folded-down seam of the bedspread, and fold the remaining spread over the pillows. Make sure to cover the pillows completely so that this looks very neat and tight—this is the final step in preparing your bed. Now, step back and admire your work. Show someone else the job you've done so that they can pat you on the back.

DO PUSH-UPS AND SIT-UPS

KATHY SMITH

*

Kathy Smith is a contributing editor to Self *magazine
and has been named Healthy America Fitness Leader
by the National Fitness Leaders Association in
conjunction with the President's Council on Physical
Fitness. She is also a member of the Video Hall of
Fame. She is the author of numerous books, including*
Kathy Smith's Lift Weights to Lose Weight.

PUSH-UPS

The fact is, your *arms* may know how to do a push-up, but doing
it properly is something you have to teach your entire body. The
key to the perfect push-up is *alignment*. Your body should be held
in a rigid, straight line—like a plank of wood—and move up and
down without bowing or sagging. To do a push-up well, you need
to focus less on the arm movement and more on stabilizing muscles throughout the body.

The following is a series of preliminary steps to help you focus on your alignment and develop the body awareness to do the push-ups with correct form.

1. Stand 2 to 3 feet from a wall with legs shoulder-width apart. (Standing adjacent to a mirror will help you judge your alignment.)
2. Place your palms on the wall, slightly below shoulder height, fingers pointed upward.
3. Contract your quadriceps to lift your kneecaps. Release and reengage 5 times, to get the feel of this action.
4. Now contract your inner thighs, as though you were trying to slide your feet together. Again, release and reengage these muscles 5 times.
5. Contract the muscles of your buttocks. Squeeze and release 5 times.
6. Elongate your torso by lifting the chest and pulling your belly toward your spine. Do this 5 times.
7. Pull your shoulders down, away from your ears, and pull your shoulder blades together in back, as though you were trying to pinch a pencil between them. Again, 5 reps.
8. Now, contract each of these areas in sequence—quadriceps, inner thighs, buttocks, stomach, chest, and shoulder blades—and hold them until *all* are engaged. Tightly holding all these stabilizers and keeping your body in a straight line, bend at the elbows and bring your body to the wall. Memorize the sensation of stability and alignment.

Doing push-ups against a wall is intended for learning purposes only. Once you have the feel for how to hold your body straight, try the same move with your hands on the back of a sturdy table top or railing—and, eventually, on the floor.

Two common mistakes are leading with the belly and "nose diving" with your butt in the air. To avoid these, simply maintain good standing posture throughout the move. Your head should be in a neutral position, in line with the rest of your spine. To help achieve this, look at a spot about 5 inches in front of you. To avoid leading with your head, place a small pillow under your chest and let that be the first point of contact as you lower yourself.

Always do only as many repetitions as you can with good form.

THE PERFECT SIT-UP

Standard sit-ups don't effectively target the stomach muscles and, worse, place unnecessary stress on the lower spine. Fortunately, the traditional sit-up has evolved into a safer and more effective variation known as the *crunch*. The crunch is designed to target the *rectus abdominis*, the uppermost of the 4 abdominal muscle layers. If you train consistently, assuming you do some aerobic exercise and watch your diet, crunches are a great way to build the coveted "six-pack." Here's how:

1. Lie on your back and draw your knees up until your feet rest flat on the floor. Your feet should be about hip distance apart and about 2 feet below your sit bones.
2. Clasp your hands behind your head.

3. Very slowly raise your shoulders and upper back about 30 degrees from the floor. Curl your upper body forward as though you're trying to touch your chin to your navel.
4. At the same time as your shoulders curl forward, let your pelvis rock upward slightly; visualize the tip of your tailbone and your ribs drawing together.
5. Keep your legs, arms, and neck relaxed throughout the motion.
6. Hold for about 1 second and release.
7. Work up to two sets of 15 repetitions. When crunches become too easy, you can increase the challenge by holding a weight to your chest or behind your head.

Now, I want to point out that precisely *because* crunches are such a great isolation exercise, they shouldn't be the only abdominal work you do. By supplementing your crunches with some form of core training, such as yoga or Pilates, you can augment that sexy firm stomach or six-pack with a host of benefits, including better posture, a slimmer appearance, more graceful movement, and improved sports performance.

*

4

JOG

GRETE WAITZ

*

Grete Waitz is a nine-time winner of the New York
Marathon and five-time World Cross-Country
Champion. She has held world
records for the 3000M, 10K, and Marathon.
She won a silver medal in the 1984 Olympics.

EQUIPMENT

1. While jogging 1 mile, each foot will land on the ground about
   1,000 times. That's a lot of pounding. If you are not wearing
   the right shoes, you might injure yourself. The pair of sneakers
   you bought 5 or 10 years ago won't do. Find a running store
   where the staff is specially trained and can advise on the
   perfect shoe for your needs. If the shoes are not comfortable in
   the store, don't buy them. Shoes don't "break in."

2. The proper jogging gear for summer is a T-shirt or singlet
   and a pair of shorts. Make sure the material is lightweight and

breathable. This will help you stay cool on warm days. On cold days you need a long-sleeved T-shirt, tights or trackster-type bottoms, and a windbreaker. And maybe a hat and a pair of lightweight gloves.

PLANNING

It is important that you start out with a program that matches your fitness level and fits your lifestyle. Many of you will have to get fit by walking before you even think of jogging. That is why walking and jogging are such great activities, because they can be easily adjusted to your needs.

Some tips before starting: Take the necessary steps to make your commitment work. Set aside time 3 days a week. Find a friend, the right time of the day, and the right attitude—anything that helps you along the road.

You should always be able to carry on a conversation while you're walking/jogging—if you can't, you are going too fast and should slow down.

TECHNIQUE

1. Jog with your shoulders back and your arms and hands relaxed. Bend your elbows at your waist and keep your hands loosely cupped. Let your arms swing naturally, moving in rhythm with your body.
2. Keep your feet and knees facing forward rather than out to the sides. Employ the heel-to-toe technique, landing on the heel, and then rolling forward to the ball of the foot and pushing off from the toes.

3. Watch your stride. Don't overstride or understride. If you do, you'll feel awkward and increase the likelihood of injuring yourself.

4. Breathe in a relaxed way through your mouth and nose. Keep your body loose and fluid. As you jog more frequently, your style will naturally become more flowing.

5. Take care on hills. When jogging downhill, don't lean backward. Keep your body at the same angle as you do when jogging on a flat surface. Jogging uphill will naturally shorten your stride, so concentrate on using your arm swing to help power you up.

6. If you want to start jogging on a treadmill, make sure you put it on a 1.5 percent incline. This duplicates the road more closely and gives you a better workout. If possible, have a mirror in front of the treadmill so you can check your form.

7. Try to jog on soft surfaces such as dirt or grass. The impact of these surfaces is gentler on your legs and joints than concrete.

8. Change your routes. Avoid jogging the same course or same direction on a track or circular path. Alternating the stress and impact will help you avoid injury and build fitness. Try to jog on varied terrain—hilly as well as flat.

9. Warm up before and cool down after. Do this by walking a few hundred yards before and after you jog.

5

EAT RIGHT

Joy Bauer

✳

*Joy Bauer, MS, RD, CDN, was named New York's best
nutritionist by* New York *magazine. She is author of*
The 90/10 Weight Loss Plan, The Complete Idiot's Guide
to Total Nutrition, *and* Cooking with Joy.

TOP TEN STRATEGIES FOR EATING SMART

1. LOAD UP ON VEGETABLES

Veggies are full of vitamins and minerals, phytochemicals (plant substances that fight disease), and fiber, which promotes regularity, lowers cholesterol, and helps stabilize blood sugar levels. And veggies are low in calories, too! Aim for at least 3 servings—½ cup cooked or 1 cup raw—every day.

2. AIM FOR 2 FRUITS PER DAY

Like veggies, fruits offer plenty of phytochemicals, fiber, vitamins, and minerals. Their high water and fiber contents help fill you up so you have less room for fatty, calorie-laden foods. Try to eat whole fruit instead of juice; juice comes at a much higher calorie cost.

3. CHOOSE WHOLE GRAINS

If you're used to eating bagels, sugary cereals, and white rice, you'll need to rethink your starch. The white stuff (refined grain) offers very little in the way of nutrition. Whole grains, on the other hand, contain fiber and keep you fuller longer, so you may eat less throughout the day. Incorporate whole grains like brown rice, oatmeal, couscous, whole-wheat bread, and pasta.

4. INCLUDE SKINNY PROTEINS

We need about 0.5 gram of protein per pound of body weight. Choose lean protein sources like skinless chicken and turkey breast, fish, lentils and beans, tofu and tempeh, lean red meats, egg whites, and low-fat dairy.

5. NIX BAD FATS

Saturated fat raises "bad" cholesterol in the blood more than anything else in your diet. Cut down on red meat, full-fat dairy, and baked goods that use the evil oils. Try to eat no more than 15 grams per day.

Trans fat also raises "bad" cholesterol and therefore the risk of heart disease. Limit your exposure by avoiding stick margarine, vegetable shortening, and products made with "partially hydrogenated" vegetable oils, such as many commercially prepared cookies, crackers, and cakes.

6. BOOST YOUR GOOD FATS

Not all fats are bad. *Unsaturated fat* can help lower "bad" cholesterol levels in the blood without lowering the "good" cholesterol. Good sources include olive oil, canola oil, nuts, and avocado. *Omega-3 fats* are also superstars in the fat category. The best sources of omega-3 fat are salmon, tuna, sardines, striped bass, trout, mackerel, bluefish, and herring. Shoot for 1 to 2 servings of these fish every week. Also, plant sources of omegas include flaxseed and walnuts—sprinkle them on yogurt and cereals and toss in salads.

7. FILL UP ON FIBER

There are two kinds of fiber, and they're both health-boosting power-houses.

Insoluble fiber is a boon for digestive health, preventing such maladies as constipation, diverticulosis, and hemorrhoids. You'll find it in wheat bran, whole grains, cereals, seeds, and many fruits and vegetables. *Soluble fiber* prevents wide swings in blood sugar levels, thereby prolonging energy, decreasing diabetes risk, and helping to reduce cholesterol levels. Sources include oats, beans, barley, apples, citrus fruits, and sweet potatoes. You will need to increase your water consumption as you increase your fiber intake. Overloading on fiber can cause bloating and other abdominal discomforts—and excessive amounts of fiber (generally 50 grams or more per day) can decrease the absorption of important vitamins and minerals.

*

8. PUT THE KIBOSH ON SUGAR

Unfortunately, besides providing us with energy and sweet satisfaction, sugar does a lot of not-so-nice things, too:

- *It makes us fat:* Sugar is nothing but empty calories and rarely sates our hunger, leading us to eat more.
- *It makes us tired:* When we eat excessive sugar, we get an energy rush. But then insulin is released and we experience an energy crash.

9. AVOID LIQUID CALORIES (EXCEPT FOR SKIM, LOW-FAT, AND SOY MILK)

If you drink 2 cups of coffee with half-and-half and sugar, 1 glass of orange juice, 2 cans of cola, and a glass of white wine, you're downing 627 calories per day from beverages alone! Drop the calorie-laden drinks, and you'll lose a pound every 6 days.

10. CREATE BALANCE!

Use a 90/10 food strategy—one that's 90 percent healthy and 10 percent fun. As long as you commit to eating healthy foods the majority of the time, there is room in every plan for a fun indulgence.

*

MAKE EGGS

Jean-Georges Vongerichten

*

Jean-Georges Vongerichten is the chef and owner of
fifteen restaurants in New York, Las Vegas, Hong Kong,
Chicago, Houston, Paris, the Bahamas, and Shanghai.
He has won four James Beard awards and is the author of
three cookbooks, including Simple to Spectacular: How to
Take One Basic Recipe to Four Levels of Sophistication.

TEN MINUTES, a saucepan, a whisk, some butter, and
some eggs—this is all you need to make the perfect scrambled
eggs. This recipe is for two people but you can double it. If you
have only a nonstick pan, switch the whisk for a wooden spoon
and the result will be just as good.

Combine 5 eggs, 1½ tablespoons of butter, and salt and pepper
to taste in a saucepan. Turn the heat to medium-high and begin to
beat the egg mixture with a whisk, stirring almost constantly but
not so fast that it becomes foamy.

After the butter melts, the mixture will begin to thicken, and then lump up in small curds. This will take between 3 and 8 minutes, depending on the thickness of your pan and the heat level. If the mixture begins to stick on the bottom, remove the pan from the heat for a moment, and continue to whisk. Then return it to the heat.

When the eggs become creamy, with small curds all over—not unlike loose oatmeal—they are ready. Serve them immediately so as not to overcook. Add more salt and pepper if necessary. The trick is to stop the cooking while the eggs are still very loose. You should eat them with a spoon.

This is the basic recipe. And while simple is great, you may let your imagination run and dress up those scrambled eggs by adding other ingredients (cheese, tomatoes, herbs, truffles . . .). Or top them with caviar.

Bon appétit!

*

BREW COFFEE

CECILE HUDON

✳

Cecile Hudon is the Senior
Coffee Education Specialist at Starbucks Coffee
Company, the leading retailer, roaster, and brand
of specialty coffee in the world.

THE KEY to a great cup of coffee is to start with high-quality coffee. Coffee trees grow in the equatorial region of the globe, between the Tropics of Cancer and Capricorn. There are many countries that produce coffee, and each one has a taste of its origin, some more distinctive than others. Soil, climate, elevation, weather, and surrounding plants are some of the natural influences on a coffee's flavor. After you choose your flavor—whether it is a bright and lively Latin American coffee; a big, bold, and smooth Indonesian; or a flavorful and exotic African coffee—it is time to brew it. The four fundamentals are proportion, grind, water, and freshness.

PROPORTION

The recipe for a flavorful cup of coffee is 2 tablespoons of ground coffee per 6 ounces of water. This proportion extracts the most flavor from your coffee without absorbing the negative flavors caused by overextraction. This recipe remains constant for most brewing methods. One variation is espresso brewing. When brewing espresso, a higher grind, as well as a higher proportion—7 grams to 1 ounce of water—is recommended to maximize the bean's flavor.

GRIND

The grind for your coffee should match your brewing method. What determines the grind is the time during which the water and coffee will be in contact. Espresso brewing is a quick-extraction method because the coffee and water are in contact for mere seconds. The grind should be fine. When brewing in a coffee press, water and coffee are mingling for 4 minutes or longer, and therefore the grind should be coarse.

The shape of the filter affects the flow rate of water through the coffee and therefore, the extraction rate. Automatic drip makers that have a flat-bottom filter require a grind slightly finer than a coffee press grind. And cone filters require an even finer grind than flat-bottom filters.

WATER

A cup of coffee is 98 percent water. A flavorful cup of coffee requires great-tasting water. If your water has off flavors, so will your coffee. Start with cold, filtered water and bring it to a temperature just off a boil, between 195 and 205 degrees Fahrenheit. Water temperature is important and is constant for all brewing methods. If your water is not hot enough, the coffee oils will not be extracted into your cup of coffee, and its inherent flavor will be lost. When purchasing a drip brewer, make sure that the brewer heats to the recommended temperature. If the brewing temperature is too hot, the coffee flavor can be scalded.

FRESHNESS

Treat your coffee like you would produce; there is an expiration date. Coffee should be consumed within 1 week of opening the package. When fresh-roasted coffee is exposed to air, light, heat, and/or moisture, its flavor starts to deteriorate. For optimum flavor, buy whole-bean coffee and grind it as needed. Once coffee is ground, more surface area is exposed and flavor deteriorates more quickly.

Buy what you'll use within 1 week's time. When storing, keep your coffee in a cool, dark place, like a kitchen cupboard. Do not store coffee in the refrigerator or the freezer. Coffee absorbs flavor, and in these environments it can absorb moisture. If you find a special coffee that you won't consume within 2 weeks and want to save for a later date, the freezer will extend the life of the unopened package for approximately 2 months for whole bean and 1 month for ground coffee.

Coffee is a universal pleasure with a diverse set of uses. It jump-starts a person's day, it ends a meal, and it is enjoyed in venues around the globe, from Austrian coffeehouses to Ethiopian coffee ceremonies, from a vending machine in Japan to your home or local coffee shop. Explore the world of coffee one cup at a time.

8

READ A NEWSPAPER

Arthur Sulzberger Jr.

✳

Arthur Sulzberger Jr. is chairman of
The New York Times Company and publisher
of The New York Times.

$\mathbf{A}$t its best, a newspaper promises to offer up all the world's news, along with some opinion, insight, and entertainment. My goal is to help you save time and, even more important, allow you to develop a guilt-free relationship with your daily broadsheet. What follows is a way for you to create your own system for extracting out of a newspaper what you want—without all those lingering doubts and fears that you are missing that one story that will bring you happiness, success, and sanity.

The starting point for your multistep, guilt-free reading program is to accept the fact that you don't need to read the newspaper in an orderly sequential fashion. It is only a question of deciding how to begin. Like swimming, there are those who like to dip in their toes and look at the headlines first. Others are plungers who pick a favorite topic and dive right into the vast ocean of newsprint. I recommend that whatever your path, you do it with a measure of conviction.

Admittedly, I begin in a conventional fashion, starting with front-page stories and then lingering over national and international reports. Given the current state of our planet, I want to know what catastrophe the human race just avoided the day before and what cataclysms might occur in the near future. Granted, having knowledge of these events can be terrifying, but also quite helpful in determining whether you need to wear your galoshes in the week ahead.

The editorial page is my next destination. It is always fun to read its current words of wisdom. The editors at most publications strongly believe they have extensive expertise on every imaginable topic under the sun . . . and even those beyond.

I also enjoy poring over readers' responses to what has just been published. Their comments are passionate and informed. My great-grandfather, Adolph Ochs, started the *New York Times*'s tradition of printing letters offering a different opinion—a radical departure from the norm at the turn of the twentieth century.

Finally, I exercise full free will, jumping from place to place, reading articles throughout the newspaper that attract my attention. It is like going to a large supermarket and seeing shelf after shelf of great stuff. You first get the necessities, but then you can follow your whim. And with newspapers, there is no additional cost—no matter how full your cart happens to get.

Now let me address the problems of those supercompulsive readers who suffer from newspaper-guilt. My suggestion, as digital archives become more commonplace, is simple: get rid of your old newspapers as fast as possible, preferably by recycling. Let's face it: if you haven't read that article in the first day or two, you are probably never going to get around to it.

Hopefully, removing some of the guilt will enhance your reading experience and help make the time that you spend with your newspaper, whether it be 10 minutes or 2 hours, more useful, more interesting, and more fun.

*

9

WASH YOUR HAIR

FRÉDÉRIC FEKKAI

✳

Frédéric Fekkai is a world-renowned celebrity stylist with his own line of luxury hair-care and body-care products. He is the owner of three salons in Beverly Hills, Palm Beach, and New York and the author of Frédéric Fekkai: A Year of Style.

GOOD HAIR can set the tone for the rest of your day. When your hair looks good, it lifts your spirits and gives you the confidence to take on any challenge. But hair, like skin, needs to be pampered to stay in shape. It all begins with these basic first steps: shampooing and conditioning.

SHAMPOOING

Most people look best if they wash their hair every day. (The exception is people with extremely thick or frizzy hair, which can sometimes be washed and blown out every few days and not touched in between.)

Too often, the nurturing products designed to go on your head end up on your scalp, where they stick like glue. For best results, never apply shampoo directly to your head. Pour the products into your hands first, and only then apply to your hair. This allows you to control how much product is applied and, most important, where it goes.

Use the right products for your hair type. Before you select your shampoo, find one that specifically addresses the needs of your hair texture:

- For dry or coarse hair, use a shampoo formulated with rich moisturizing agents.
- For damaged or overprocessed hair, use a protein shampoo.
- For thin or fine hair, choose a shampoo that will add volume and help plump up the hair shaft.
- For color-treated hair, choose an ultra-moisturizing shampoo that will cleanse and add shine without stripping the color.
- Most men should use a shampoo that contains agents to make their hair appear thicker.

Alternate shampoos several times a week to get hair to look its healthiest. For example, alternate a shampoo to address the need of your dry hair with a shampoo that will enhance your color-treated hair. There are shampoos that are designed for specific hair color(s). I also highly recommend using a shampoo that is deep cleansing to rid the hair of product buildup.

Follow these key steps to get the best out of your shampoo:

1. Saturate your hair with water before putting in any shampoo. If it isn't completely wet to the roots, the shampoo won't flow through the hair, leading to a mane that's dull or even flaky due to shampoo residues.
2. When applying shampoo, don't apply it all to the top of your head. Apply a small amount at the forehead, crown, temples, and the nape of the neck. Use a wide-tooth comb to distribute the shampoo through the hair.
3. When rinsing hair of shampoo (or conditioner), begin with warm water, then switch to the coldest water you can bear. Warm water opens the hair shaft and cold water closes it. The colder the water, the shinier the hair.

CONDITIONING

Most hair needs conditioning as regularly as it needs washing. Even very oily hair can be dry and brittle at the ends. Conditioners can restore the flexibility and prevent damage. They also help hair combat the assaults of brushes, heat appliances, and environmental factors like sun, pollution, and the cold. To find the correct conditioner, follow the above guidelines in terms of identifying your specific hair texture and needs. And keep these tips in mind for the perfect condition:

1. Never apply the product to your scalp, unless you have a very dry scalp.

2. Apply conditioner from the ears down, or the ends only on shorter hair. Only the hair you can grab into a ponytail should have product.

3. Avoid applying any product on the root area, because it will weigh the hair down, leaving it flat on top. On short hair, focus the concentration of conditioner on the ends of the hair. Comb the product through the hair, but make certain to comb from ends to roots. This motion will eliminate breakage. Rinse with cool water as you continue to comb, giving the hair even more shine.

*

10

CARE FOR YOUR SKIN

SIDRA SHAUKAT

*

Sidra Shaukat is the author of Natural Beauty: The
Natural Approach to Skin and Body Care *and*
Regenerate Yourself Younger: The Scientific Proof
for Preventing Aging and Disease.
She is the skin-care columnist for iVillage UK.

L O V E the skin you're in! Beautiful, soft skin is the ultimate beauty asset, so take good care of it. Your skin is an essential multipurpose organ, the largest in the body. The condition of your skin depends on several factors, such as your genes, age, the quality of your diet, stress, hormones, sun exposure, and smoke.

YOUR SKIN TYPE

Skin types vary from person to person, and they often change with the season, age, and other factors such as pregnancy and stress.

These are the main types:

- Normal: Lucky you! This is perfect skin—soft, smooth, and finely textured. Use gentle cleansers, moisturize daily, and use weekly face masks.
- Dry: Skin gets drier as we age, becoming tight and devoid of moisture, so adequate moisturizing becomes essential. Keep your skin away from excess temperatures. Use gentle, alcohol-free cleansers, rich moisturizers, and night creams.
- Sensitive: This skin is fine, suffers from redness and irritation, and does poorly when exposed to extremes of weather or harsh products. Extra care is needed for sensitive skin. Use cosmetics without perfume, color, alcohol, or lanolin.
- Oily: Oily skin is thicker, has large pores, looks shiny, and is prone to spots. The increased moisture production can be aggravated by stress and hormonal imbalances. Avoid harsh lotions but opt for pH-balanced cleansers and oil-free moisturizers.
- Combination: This skin is the most common, with an oily T-zone (forehead, nose, and chin) and dry cheeks and neck. Try gentle cleansers and oil-free moisturizers.

All skin types should use eye cream or gel, applied gently on the delicate eye area; lip balm; and a day cream with sunscreen. Use appropriate face scrubs and masks once a week.

SKIN-CARE TIPS

1. WHAT TO AVOID

Don'ts include: sun exposure, smoking, "yo-yo" dieting, caffeine, excess sugar, and stress.

2. HEALTHY SKIN DIET

Start caring for your skin from within:

- *Drink water:* 8 glasses of pure water throughout each day will hydrate your skin, flush toxins from your body, increase the skin's radiance, and relieve puffiness.
- *Eat protein:* Aging, sagging skin is caused by the breakdown of skin cells, which cannot self-repair without adequate protein. Protein forms strong, healthy collagen and new cell walls.
- *Essential fatty acids (EFAs):* These keep your skin soft, supple, and radiant; enhance moisture retention from within; and assist in repairing the skin's natural moisture barrier. EFAs are found in oily fish such as mackerel, trout, and salmon, and nonfish sources like avocados, seeds, and nuts.
- *Limit carbohydrates:* Your skin can age prematurely if your diet is full of refined carbohydrates such as white bread and convenience foods that are packed with preservatives. The high levels of toxicity in the skin make it puffy, dehydrated, and slack.

- *Vegetables:* Eating brightly colored fruit and vegetables will enhance your skin's metabolism and strength, reduce inflammation, and protect DNA.

3. RELAX

Laughter lines form over time in spots where muscles tend to contract. Make a conscious effort to relax any tense muscles in your face.

4. MOISTURIZE

Use moisturizer or oils such as olive oil or coconut oil to rejuvenate your skin. Moisturizing keeps the skin's connective tissues strong and supple, preventing sagging and wrinkles. Your skin releases its own natural moisturizer, which forms the skin's protective "acid mantle." Harsh soaps and cleansers strip this vital layer, leaving it exposed to infection. Cleopatra bathed in ass's milk to preserve this layer, making her skin lustrous!

5. EXFOLIATE

Daily exfoliation, preferably at night, removes the dead top layer of skin and speeds up your skin renewal process.

6. FREQUENT SPAS

Saunas and steam rooms eliminate toxins and encourage skin renewal. Jacuzzis increase circulation and skin rejuvenation.

11

SHAVE

Myriam Zaoui and Eric Malka

*

*Myriam Zaoui and Eric Malka are the
husband-and-wife co-owners of The Art of Shaving,
a line of retail stores and producer of shaving
products. They are the authors of* The Art of Shaving.

On AVERAGE, men shave 5.33 times a week—about 21,000 shaves in a lifetime. Unfortunately, many have acquired bad shaving habits that can yield unpleasant results or injuries like razor burn, ingrown hairs, and nicks and cuts. The good news is that once the right tools and products have been selected, the only thing that stands between you and an ultra-smooth, close, comfortable shave is learning the proper techniques.

Traditional wet shaving, which has been around since prehistoric times, will make the shave as smooth, close, and comfortable as possible. Wet shaving involves the use of shaving cream or soap, shaving brushes, water, and a blade. The fundamental principles of wet shaving revolve around the importance of hot water, a rich warm lather, and the actual techniques themselves.

STEP 1. PREPARE

- Always shave after or during a hot shower, never before.
- Before shaving, apply a pre-shave oil treatment to protect the skin and to soften the beard.
- Always use hot water while shaving. It softens the beard, opens pores, and cleanses the skin.

STEP 2. LATHER

- Use a glycerin-based shaving cream or shaving soap. Avoid foams, gels, or other products that contain numbing agents such as benzocaine or menthol, which tend to close pores and stiffen the beard.
- For best results, use a shaving brush made of badger hair. It softens and lifts the beard from the face and helps generate a warm and rich lather.

STEP 3. SHAVE

- Select a clean, sharp blade and dip it in hot water.
- Always shave with the grain first—that is, in the direction the hair grows. Shaving against the grain can cause ingrown hairs and razor burn. For an even closer shave, relather and shave lightly across or against the grain.
- Check to see whether the hair on your neck grows in the same direction as the hair on your face. If it doesn't, make sure you adjust accordingly to shave with the grain.

- Use a razor with a weighted handle to provide proper weight, balance, and comfort for better control.
- Avoid applying too much pressure on your razor since this is often the cause of razor burn and skin irritations. Glide the razor gently over your face.

STEP 4. MOISTURIZE

- After shaving, apply an alcohol-free moisturizing aftershave balm or aftershave gel to nourish, soothe, and moisten the skin. Avoid aftershaves that contain alcohol; these can irritate and dry out the skin and cause ingrown hairs.
- In the event of nicks or cuts, use an alum block or a styptic pen to stop the bleeding.

✳

12

APPLY LIPSTICK

BOBBI BROWN

*

Bobbi Brown is the CEO of Bobbi Brown Cosmetics,
and a New York Times *bestselling author.*

LIPSTICK is the quickest and easiest way to instantly look pulled-together. And it's the perfect way to test the waters if you're a makeup novice. Start by finding a basic shade that looks great on you even when you're bare-faced. For most women, it's a shade that looks like the natural color of their lips taken up a few notches. Once you have this everyday basic, you can try different colors and textures to fit your mood and the occasion. Here's a lipstick how-to with everything you need to know to get perfectly made-up lips.

- Start with clean, smooth lips. If they're chapped, smooth some eye cream onto your lips, then use a toothbrush or a washcloth to gently exfoliate them and get rid of dry skin.

- Lipstick comes in a handful of formulas with different degrees of coverage and wear. Pick the formula based on your needs and your style. *Matte:* This has the most coverage and the longest wear. Some matte formulas can be drying, so look for a semi-matte version that's creamy. *Shimmer:* This formula combines color with light-reflecting pigments. Look for sheer finishes and stay away from overly frosted formulas. *Stain:* Transparent color that's practically mistake proof. A good bet for beginners.

- Neutral colors and sheer formulas can be applied directly from the tube. Start at the center of the top lip, working your way out to the corners. Repeat with the bottom lip. Finish by blotting lips together to blend.

- A lip brush is your best bet for darker or brighter colors—and especially matte formulas—that require precise application. The bristles of the lip brush should be firm, but bend easily as lipstick is applied. Look for a brush head that's flat and comes to a slight point.

- Using the lip brush, apply lipstick on the center of the top lip and work your way out to the corners. Use short strokes, brushing color in thin, even layers. Make sure to follow the natural shape of your lip. Repeat with the bottom lip. If you want more intensity, apply a second layer of lipstick to both top and bottom lips.

- A lip pencil applied after lipstick gives lips subtle definition and keeps color from feathering. If your lipstick is neutral, look for a nude shade of pencil that blends in with your natural lip color. If your lipstick is dark or bright, look for a lip pencil that's one shade deeper.

- When lining lips, make sure the pencil tip is softly rounded, and hold the pencil at a slight angle. Follow the natural shape of your lips and keep your strokes soft, with no sharp angles. If needed, use a lip brush to soften the edges.
- To make lipstick longer wearing, line and fill in lips with the lip pencil, then apply lipstick.
- Experiment by mixing different shades of lipstick to create new colors. A beige lipstick can tone down an overly bright shade. A blackberry lipstick can deepen your daytime color and turn it into a great evening shade. On days when you don't feel like wearing lipstick and want a low-maintenance look, pair lip balm with lip pencil. And in a pinch, lipstick makes a great cream blush!

*

13

WASH YOUR HANDS

JULIE GERBERDING

*

Dr. Julie Gerberding is the director of the Centers for
Disease Control and Prevention (CDC), an agency of the
U.S. Department of Health and Human Services. The
CDC is recognized as the lead federal agency for
protecting the health and safety of the American people.

ONE OF the most important things that you can do to keep from getting sick is to wash your hands. Every one of us is constantly picking up germs from other sources, and then we infect ourselves when we touch our eyes, nose, or mouth. By frequently washing or cleaning your hands, you eliminate germs that you have picked up from other people, animals, or contaminated surfaces. The important thing to remember is that, in addition to colds, some pretty serious diseases—like hepatitis A or meningitis—may be prevented if people make a habit of washing their hands. Here's how:

1. Wet your hands.
2. Apply either a liquid or bar soap.
3. Rub your hands together vigorously to make a lather and scrub all surfaces (including between your fingers and under your fingernails).
4. Continue to rub your hands together for 20 seconds. It takes that long for the soap and scrubbing action to dislodge and remove stubborn germs. Need a timer? Imagine singing "Happy Birthday" twice.
5. Rinse your hands well under running water.
6. Dry your hands using a paper towel or air dryer.
7. If possible, use your paper towel to turn off the faucet.

If soap and water are not available, consider using an alcohol-based handrub to clean your hands. You should wash your hands often, probably more often than you do now, because you can't see germs with the naked eye. It is especially important to wash your hands:

- Before, during, and after you prepare food
- Before you eat
- After you use the bathroom
- After handling animals or animal waste
- When you or someone in your home is sick
- When your hands are dirty

Encourage those around you to wash their hands too. It will help increase your chances of avoiding germs.

14

SHINE SHOES

SAL IACONO

✳

*Sal Iacono, aka the Sole Man, owns Continental Shoe
Repair, just steps from New York's City Hall. He has shined
numerous mayors' shoes and currently is the shoe shiner for
Mayor Michael Bloomberg and many of Wall Street's elite.*

YOU DON'T need to be a genius to shine shoes, but the first
key is recognizing that there's a distinct difference between shining
and cleaning. For example, it is impossible to shine white shoes—
no matter what kind of leather. You can, however, clean them with
a variety of different cleaners and/or a white cream.

If you scratch a pair of white shoes, polish doesn't help. You
need to use a white spray to cover the spot. You should not polish
beige or tan shoes either. Polish may give you a shine, but it does
not clean scratches or stains. Light-colored shoes need to be
cleaned, and the color reconditioned, by using a spray, available at
your local shoemaker.

When dealing with black, brown, medium, or dark shades of shoe, the technique is quite simple. Begin by removing the dust from the shoes using a regular towel. If you have mud on the hedge—the continuous edge—of the shoes, use a damp cloth to get rid of the muck.

Once the dust, dirt, and mud are removed, it's time to clean—but not yet polish—the shoe. Work with a cleaner (liquid, cream, or paste) that matches the color of the shoes. Apply the cleaner with a shoeshine rag, which comes in three dimensions: small, medium, and large. (For a person with regular hands, a medium rag should be used. But a shiner with big hands should use a large rag, which gives more control over the cleaning of the shoe.) A soft hand towel can be used as the shoeshine rag, or you can go to a store and request a cloth made specifically for shoe shining. Once the cleaner is applied, use strong, fluid motions to work the rag up and down the length of the shoe, spreading the cleaner evenly throughout. This should take about two minutes.

Brush off the cleaner with a horsehair brush. The combination of the rag followed by the brush brings up the shine. Never use a nylon brush, which will spoil the leather and never give you a good shine.

When cleaning the hedge, use the Sole Dresser reconditioning product. If you want an even brighter shine, apply Kiwi polish and work with the same technique.

As for polishing, the last step of the process, you can use a rag, but a small round-shaped brush is preferred because it makes the polish easier to apply and helps keep it off your hands. It also gives you more control over the amount of polish used, and so provides a more even polish.

In total, a solid shoe shine should take about 7 to 10 minutes.

15

TIE A BOW TIE

Tucker Carlson

*

Tucker Carlson is the co-host of CNN's Crossfire *and
the author of* Politicians, Partisans, and Parasites:
My Adventures in Cable News. *He has worn
bow ties exclusively since the ninth grade.*

HERE are my tips for tying a bow tie:

1. Buy or borrow a bow tie. Silk ties are easier for beginners,
   though cotton ties will work. Use chalk or
   washable ink to write the letter "A" on
   one end, "B" on the other. (Indelible ink
   is suitable only for borrowed ties.)
2. Drape the bow tie around your collar.
   Place A over B. Make certain that A, the
   front end of the tie, is an inch or so longer
   than B.

3. Fold B in half, into the shape of a bow. Hold against your neck with one hand.

4. This is the tricky part. With your other hand, bring A straight down, bisecting B. Place the thumb of the hand that is holding B into the center of A. Push the center of A behind B at the folded end. Pull through.

5. Tighten by pulling on the opposite folded ends. Adjust by fiddling. This is the subjective, artistic phase of the process. You may opt for the loose, floppy, glass-of-cognac-in-the-morning Churchill look; the precision-perfect Fruit of Islam, Farrakhan-bodyguard look; or somewhere in between. As in life, somewhere in between is probably best.

6. Admire handicraft in mirror.

7. Consider whether you really want to do this. Keep in mind that when you wear a bow tie, people will make assumptions about you, and probably should. The good news is, you'll never commit adultery when you wear a bow tie; you won't have the opportunity. The bad news is, strangers will snicker at you in airports. Is it worth it? Only you can be the judge.

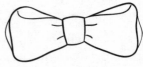

16

TIE A WINDSOR KNOT

THUY TRANTHI

*

*Thuy Tranthi is president of Thomas Pink
North America.*

I N the 1930s, the Duke of Windsor, known for his sartorial elegance, started the trend for the Windsor knot, and it has remained a popular knot to this day. Part of its appeal is its look, which is more substantial than the ordinary and more commonly used four-in-hand. It is a knot that makes a statement and projects confidence and style.

The Windsor knot's defining characteristic is its symmetry, resulting from the wide tie end wrapped twice around the neck loop. Because it is a thicker knot, the Windsor should be worn with a spread collar.

The rituals of tying a tie should be followed as you prepare for tying a classic Windsor knot. Rushing through the process may yield unfortunate results and, more important, will diminish the pleasure of indulging in a moment of pampering.

Put your tie on in front of a mirror to see what you're doing during each step. The mirror will enable you to determine the correct length of your tie as well as the proper positioning of your tie against the collar. Always button up your shirt all the way, including the collar, and stand the collar up before draping the tie around your neck.

As a general rule, the wide end of your tie should hang twice as low as the narrow end. And because it's the part you'll be working with the most, you should let it hang on the side of your dominant hand to make the process easier.

How to tie a Windsor knot in ten easy steps:

1. Cross the wide end over the narrow end to the left and bring it from behind to the front, up and through the neck loop.
2. Pull the wide end down and wrap it behind to the right.
3. Wrap the wide end up, in front, and over the neck loop, where the knot is forming, so that the back side shows and extends to the left.
4. Loop the wide end horizontally and to the right, in front of the knot that is being created.

STEP #1   STEP #2

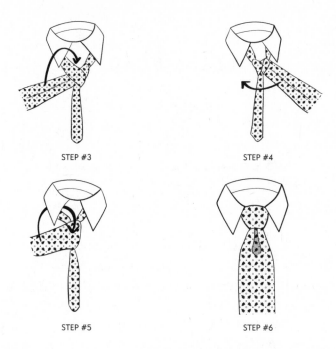

STEP #3   STEP #4

STEP #5   STEP #6

5. Bring the widened end from behind, up through the neck loop.
6. Tuck it through the front loop that was just formed.
7. Tighten the knot and draw it up to the collar.
8. Turn down the collar over the tie.
9. Adjust the knot so that it sits squarely in the middle of the collar.
10. Ensure that the tie reaches down to the waistband.

Now, stand back and admire the results—or, better yet, go out and have others admire your sartorial splendor.

17

TIE A SCARF

NICOLE MILLER

*

Nicole Miller designs her own fashion line and owns
twenty boutiques bearing her name.

$\mathbf{S}$ **CARVES** come in many colors, sizes, and shapes—the standard scarf, the pocket square, the oblong scarf. It's the perfect accessory for any occasion, even the unexpected situations that take you by surprise. A scarf can take you from the beach to a dance club in just a few simple steps.

COVER-UP OR SARONG

For a cover-up or sarong, fold your scarf in half, either side to side (forming a rectangle) or corner to corner (forming a triangle); then wrap the long side around your waist and tie the corners in a knot.

HALTER TOP

When you are ready to show off your golden tan (or crisp sunburn), fold the scarf in half to form a triangle and tie a knot with the corners of the long side. Simply slip the knot over your head and separate the two points on the bottom, then pull them around your waist, tying them in the front or back—now you have a beautiful halter top that shows off your shoulders.

HEAD

Everyone needs a basic head covering from time to time, whether to prevent a bad hair day, or to keep others from noticing an already bad hair day. Start by folding a square scarf corner to corner to form a triangle, then fold the long side over toward the opposite point to make it the right size for your head. Rest the triangle on your head (with the point facing your back), then pull the ends to the back of your head and tie them either on top of or under your hair. For a secure shield against the wind when driving a hot little convertible, use the same technique but wrap the ends around your neck once before tying in a tight knot under your chin.

When you are more concerned with being inconspicuous, just rest the triangle on your head in the same manner and tie the ends down in a loose knot under your chin so that the front slightly hides the sides of your face. The disguise works best when accompanied by massive opaque sunglasses; however, be forewarned you may in fact become more mysterious and intriguing. And if you're more Thelma and Louise than hounded icon, place the scarf firmly on your head, tie all three corners of the triangle around the base of your ponytail, and ride off into the sunset on your Harley.

NECK

Whether you have a square or oblong scarf, either can be used as a fabulous neck decoration and warmer. For a Parisian look, use a square scarf. Fold it into a triangle and then roll the long side toward the short side until it becomes ropelike. Then wrap it around your neck with a chic knot on the side, add a beret, and cry, *"Bonjour, mes amis!"*

An oblong scarf can be draped around your neck with the ends falling down your back for an elegant evening look. Or fold it in half, place it around the back of your neck, and pull the side with the two scarf ends through the closed loop for a more secure muffler on a chilly fall day.

OTHER USES

Your scarf might also come through in a pinch. If your strapless evening gown is leaving you a shivering (albeit gorgeous) guest at an air-conditioned gala, make a fabulous wrap from a large scarf by folding it into a triangle and draping it over your shoulders and arms. And if a male guest calls on you unexpectedly while you are less than fully clothed, wrap a large scarf around you and tie it in front for a makeshift robe more subtly provocative than Holly Golightly's button-down man's shirt.

Happy scarving!

18

DRIVE A STICK SHIFT

TINA GORDON

*

*Tina Gordon is a NASCAR Craftsman
Truck Series driver.*

I CAN remember trying to drive my first stick shift. I was fourteen years old, and it was my older brother's pickup truck. He was afraid I was going to tear the clutch out of his truck. But learning how to drive a stick that young really helped me with my racing career, since all race cars are stick shifts. Here's how to do it:

1. MAKE SURE YOU ARE COMFORTABLE IN THE CAR

You may want to sit a little closer to the wheel than usual because you need to use your left foot to push the clutch to the floorboard.

2. PRACTICE WITHOUT THE ENGINE RUNNING

Learn the shift pattern through practice. Use the clutch and shift gears without the engine running.

3. START IN FIRST GEAR

Push the clutch all the way to the floor and then start the engine. The hardest part is getting the car to move. Give the engine just a little gas and slowly let out the clutch into first gear. Expect to stall the car multiple times and endure laughter from anyone who is watching. Just remember, most people make the same stalling mistake when they are trying to learn.

4. PRACTICE STARTING AND STOPPING

You did it! The car is moving and you feel great. But before you try shifting to another gear, practice starting and stopping until you get proficient. To stop, let off the gas and push in the clutch at the same time. With the clutch still depressed with your left foot, apply the brake with your right foot.

5. SHIFT UP FROM FIRST GEAR

To shift into second gear, let off the gas, push in the clutch, and shift. Make sure you let off the gas so as not to over-rev the engine. Most cars have tachometers so you can watch your RPMs (revolutions per minute): on most cars, if you stay between 2500 and 3000 RPMs, you will be safe.

Shift up to the next gear when you have increased your speed by about 12 to 15 mph. For example, shift from first to second gear at 15 mph; shift from second to third gear at 30 mph; and so on. After you have driven a stick shift a few times, shifting at the right speed will begin to come naturally.

6. DOWNSHIFT TO STOP

Now it is time to stop the car. We stop by downshifting. One of the fun parts of being able to drive a stick shift is to anticipate a corner or hill and start downshifting. Downshifting is like upshifting: let off the gas, press on the clutch, and shift from fourth gear to third, third to second, and second to first.

Do not apply the brakes while downshifting from fourth through second, because lower gears will slow the car naturally. But do apply the brakes when you are in first gear. The exception to this rule is if you are about to hit something. In that case, stand hard on the brakes at any gear, pray, and close your eyes!

7. PARK

Finally, when parking a stick shift, park the car in first gear, or reverse, and always use the parking brake.

*

WORK
LIFE

19

MANAGE YOUR TIME

STEPHEN R. COVEY

*

Dr. Stephen R. Covey is the author of numerous books,
including The 7 Habits of Highly Effective People.
He is co-founder and vice-chairman of FranklinCovey
Company, a global professional services firm.

I N M Y experience, most time-management struggles or fail-
ures have less to do with skill and techniques, and more to do with
people not developing a vision and commitment toward the most
important things in their lives—including the principles they
want their lives to be built upon. Effective time management,
then, is really about *life leadership* and involves a four-step process:

1. WRITE A PERSONAL MISSION STATEMENT
A personal mission statement embodies the principles you stand
for and your vision of your life. Take time to consider those things
and relationships you value the most—that bring you a sense of
meaning, purpose, peace, happiness, and fulfillment. Think about

the principles that will produce the quality of life you seek. Without such anchoring vision, we will inevitably spend our days in the "thick of thin things"—straining under the "tyranny of the urgent."

2. IDENTIFY THE 5 TO 7 MAIN ROLES OF YOUR LIFE

Your roles may include mother, father, wife, husband, vice president of marketing, product manager, committee chairman, friend/ neighbor, PTA member, church volunteer. As you think about these roles, you may want to expand your mission statement.

3. SET GOALS FOR EACH ROLE

Do think about long-term yearly goals, but at the beginning of each week, review your mission and roles and set goals for each role, scheduling time to accomplish them during that week.

4. LIVE WITH INTEGRITY TO YOUR VISION, ROLES, AND GOALS

By *integrity* I mean your ability to make and keep commitments. The key to strengthening personal integrity and discipline is to start small. The best place for most of us to begin is with our body. If you have difficulty arising when the alarm goes off in the morning, commit to retiring at a reasonable hour and arising early for one week. Then commit to another week—then a month. Each time you make one of these small commitments and keep it, you increase your power to make and keep greater ones. Then expand your personal commitment to exercising so many times a week. Continue the next week. Next you might make a commitment regarding your diet and eating habits or perhaps a reading program.

As you continue to make and keep promises to yourself and others, you will find that your power to live with integrity to your mission and vision becomes greater than your moods. Ignoring or procrastinating what is most important to you in the long run would be like trading your diamonds for dust.

As we take time each week to reflect on the few most important roles in our life, and what we would like to accomplish in those roles, we begin to access a powerful inner compass. It is the inner compass of our heart, mind, and spirit that gives us both wisdom and guidance about how to serve and fulfill the needs of those about whom we care most—a spouse, child, friend, neighbor, colleague. It is the inner compass that gives us direction and power to keep commitments, prioritize successfully, inspire us to rise above selfishness, petty smallness, laziness, and indifference, and move us toward our tremendous potential. It is the inner compass that enables us to say no to the good or less-than-good and say yes to the best. It is the inner compass that enables us to know when to depart from the planned and scheduled things of our lives in favor of a more important need of the moment.

The more we notice and follow the indicators this magnificent inner compass gives us, the stronger and clearer the direction of the compass toward true-north principles becomes. May we all become aware of the great power of this compass and remember that compasses are most effective when we take a few moments to stop running and be still.

20

ORGANIZE

JULIE MORGENSTERN

*

*Julie Morgenstern is founder and owner of the
professional organizing firm Julie Morgenstern's Task
Masters. She is the author of three books, including*
Organizing from the Inside Out, *and is a columnist
with* O: The Oprah Magazine.

CREATING A CLUTTER-FREE S.P.A.C.E.

Ready to get organized, but don't know where to start? Whether cleaning out a closet, kitchen cabinet, or garage, follow my S.P.A.C.E. formula to make the task manageable, methodical, and rewarding. The key to succeeding with the S.P.A.C.E. formula is to do *every one of* the steps and, most important, to do them *in order.* Attack and complete one room at a time for the biggest sense of accomplishment and success.

SORT

No matter what you are organizing—from papers to clothes to sports equipment—start by grouping similar items to see what you have. Clear a space on the floor, begin in one corner, and circle the room, putting each item into a category. Resist the urge to focus on throwing things out right away. It's much easier to decide what to keep and what to toss once you have some perspective on how much you've accumulated in each category.

PURGE

Going pile by pile, review the contents, asking yourself of each item: "Do I use this? Do I love this?" If you answer yes to either question, keep it. If no, out it goes. Most of us use only about 20 percent of everything we own—that is, we wear the same 20 percent of our clothing, refer back to the same 20 percent of our files, and listen to the same 20 percent of our CDs over and over again. Still, purging is the toughest step. To make it easier, keep the following in mind:

- Toss the "No-Brainers": These are items that are obviously in such bad shape and so irrelevant to your current life that you'd never dream of using them—for example, dried-up pens; stained, torn, or pilled clothing; and rusty safety pins.
- Adopt a Charity or Friend: Give away items you bought long ago but have never actually used—no matter how much you spent on them! It's much easier to part with things if they're going to a person or organization you care about.
- Focus on the Payoff You'll Glean from Lightening Your Load: *Space* for the things you really use and love; *Time* lost from searching through all the clutter; *Money* that the

clutter is costing you; and *Satisfaction* by sharing the items you never use with the world.

ASSIGN A HOME

Decide precisely *where* you're going to store each category of keepers. Be specific—which shelf, which drawer, which section of the rod, which side of the bed? Keep frequency of use, accessibility, and logical sequencing in mind. For example, workout wear might make sense next to bathing suits, dress shirts next to blazers.

CONTAINERIZE

Containers allow you to personalize and beautify your system. By waiting until this stage to go shopping, you'll be sure to get the exact containers you need. Make a list, measure the spaces your containers must fit into, and take your tape measure to the store. Label the containers to make it easy for you to remember what goes where.

EQUALIZE

Once your system is in place, design a simple maintenance program. A well-organized room takes no more than five minutes to clean up at the end of each day, no matter how messy it gets. Annual "tune-ups" will ensure that your system keeps pace (equalizes) with your changing needs, possessions, and priorities.

21

HANDLE A JOB INTERVIEW

TORY JOHNSON

*

Tory Johnson is the founder and CEO of Women For
Hire and the co-author of Women For Hire:
The Ultimate Guide to Getting a Job.

LANDING a job interview is only half the battle; you still have
to handle it effectively. These six straightforward steps will prepare you to master the process.

1. BE A DETECTIVE

Find out everything you can about the interviewer and his or her
organization. When was the company started, and where is it
headed? Determine who the company's competitors are, its target
market, and the niche it serves. Read media coverage to see how
the press perceives the company. If it keeps a low profile, or has
none at all, what does that indicate?

2. DO YOUR HOMEWORK

In advance of the interview, ask for a copy of the full job description and prepare talking points that illustrate how you meet and

exceed the criteria. Make lists of your knowledge, skills, and abilities along with supporting examples to impress the interviewer with your accomplishments. Rehearse answers to the typical interview questions with a friend you can trust to provide honest feedback. ("Tell me about yourself" and "What are your strengths? Weaknesses? Areas for development?") Never answer the "What is your greatest weakness?" question with a negative, such as "I'm terrible at cold-calling." Instead, try using a positive like "I'm taking a course now to enhance my cold-calling skills." Have a list of anecdotes at the ready so, for example, when you're asked about a time when you had to satisfy an unhappy client, you can answer confidently.

3. PACK YOUR BAG

Your résumé must be flawless—grammatically correct with no spelling errors or typos. Your résumé should detail all of your accomplishments and highlight how, for example, you've increased sales, improved quality, streamlined operations, or enhanced productivity. The more you can quantify, the better. Bring a portfolio of your work and be prepared to leave it for review. Have a list of references with you, including names, contact information, and a sentence or two on your professional connection with each person. Get permission from these people to give out their names, and be absolutely confident they'll sing your praises.

4. BE A RAY OF LIGHT

Let your personality shine. Connect with your interviewer on a "human level." If he mentions just returning from vacation, show a genuine interest in his travels. Ask questions about her experiences at the company, such as her history there and what she likes about her position. Without going overboard, turn on the charm, and always smile.

5. STEPS TO SUCCESS

To avoid being left in the dark, confirm the next steps in the hiring process before leaving the interview. Who's the point person? How will you be contacted—by phone or e-mail? Will there be another round of interviews? Will you need to make a presentation or take any skills-assessment tests? By what date would they hope to fill the position? Learn as much as you can about what to expect.

6. IT'S NOT OVER YET

Follow-up is key. E-mail a thank you immediately after the interview, and then send a handwritten note. Thank-yous should not be sent as a mass e-mail, so personalize and individualize them and confirm the proper spelling of names and titles. Follow up with the point person on the date agreed upon and ask if there is any additional information you can provide to aid in the decision-making process. If you are offered and accept a position, congratulations! Send yet another thank-you note to the interviewers letting them know you look forward to working with them. If you have not been offered the position, never burn a bridge by showing bitterness or anger over the rejection. Instead, ask for constructive feedback that may help you going forward, and ask to keep the lines of communication open in the event of future needs.

22

ASK FOR A RAISE
OR PROMOTION

LEE E. MILLER

*   *   *

Lee E. Miller is the managing director of
NegotiationPlus.com, the author of Get More Money on
Your Next Job, *and co-author, with his daughter Jessica,*
of A Woman's Guide to Successful Negotiating. *He has*
also produced an interactive training CD entitled
NegotiationPlus 101: The Art of Getting What You Want.

1. WHEN SEEKING A RAISE, TIMING IS IMPORTANT. You
don't just wake up one morning and ask for a raise or a promotion.
You have to prepare well in advance and lay the groundwork first.

**2. MOST BOSSES DON'T KNOW WHAT YOU DO ON A DAILY
BASIS, SO YOU HAVE TO COMMUNICATE YOUR SUCCESSES
IN A VARIETY OF WAYS.** When you have an opportunity to talk
to your boss about other matters, casually mention your most
recent achievements. For example, "By the way, I thought you

might want to know we just completed the mega project, and our client was pleased."

3. A GOOD WAY TO LET YOUR BOSS KNOW ABOUT YOUR SUC-CESSES IS TO SHARE THE CREDIT WITH YOUR SUBORDINATES. Telling your boss what a great job your team did enables you to brag all you want without looking like you are.

4. HAVING REGULARLY COMMUNICATED YOUR ACCOMPLISH-MENTS, YOU CAN NOW SELECT THE APPROPRIATE MOMENT TO BROACH THE TOPIC OF A RAISE OR A PROMOTION. To ask, though, you need a reason. "I have not had a raise in a while" is not a reason. "I just completed my MBA"; "I have been your top producer over the past 6 months"; "I took over additional responsibilities and have handled them without a hitch"; "I have a job offer from your biggest competitor"—those are reasons.

5. IF YOU CAN'T FIND A REASON, CREATE ONE. Unless your last name happens to be Hilton, no one is going to hand you a raise or a promotion without a reason. Doing something that makes your boss look good to his superiors creates an opportunity to bring up a salary increase. Learning new skills and seeking and handling additional responsibility also serve this purpose.

6. THE BEST JUSTIFICATION FOR A RAISE IS HAVING ANOTHER JOB OFFER. Even if you like your job, you should periodically test your market value by quietly exploring other opportunities. Once you get an offer, you are in an excellent position to discuss salary.

7. HAVING CHOSEN AN OPPORTUNE MOMENT, YOU ARE NOW READY TO SIT DOWN AND TALK ABOUT A RAISE OR PROMOTION. Make an appointment to meet with your boss under the premise of discussing your career rather than your salary, because your boss will likely be as eager to talk salary as he is to have a root canal.

8. WHEN YOU MEET WITH YOUR BOSS, SEEK ADVICE RATHER THAN ASKING DIRECTLY. Review the reasons you feel deserving of a raise or a promotion and ask what else you will need to do. By asking for advice, you avoid being adversarial, and it will be harder to deny your request. Either your boss will begin the process of getting you a raise or promotion, or you will be told what you need to do to get one, in which case you should keep your boss informed of your progress so that he remains invested in the process.

9. IF YOU HAVE ANOTHER JOB OFFER, TELL YOUR BOSS ABOUT IT. Emphasize that you like working for the company and for your boss, but that the offer is for substantially more money and/or has greater career potential. Ask your boss what she would do. If your boss is not prepared to get you a raise, you need to be prepared to leave.

Remember that, over time, even a small raise will be valuable because all future raises, bonuses, and retirement benefits will be based on your new salary.

23

GIVE AND RECEIVE
A COMPLIMENT

MARY MITCHELL

*

Mary Mitchell is president of The Mitchell Organization, a Philadelphia-based training and consulting firm that helps corporations and individuals hone their personal interaction skills. She is iVillage's social skills expert and the author of five books, including The Complete Idiot's Guide to Etiquette *and* Class Acts: How Good Manners Create Good Relationships and Good Relationships Create Good Business. *She is also known as the nationally syndicated columnist Ms. Demeanor.*

WHATEVER their subject—our svelte new figure, our rousing speech, or our fabulous meal—compliments lift us, honor us, validate our choices and efforts. A compliment is a two-way gift that benefits giver and recipient alike. Compliments are *always* socially proper, if sincerely extended and kept appropriate to the context. (More on this later.)

If someone always looks great, tell him or her. If someone is always efficient, acknowledge that. Compliments can break the ice with a stranger, defuse stress, lift spirits, or tighten a bond. The right words at the right time can motivate, comfort, reward, validate, and inspire.

Compliments are not the same as flattery. Flattery is insincere and excessive. Superfluous compliments are annoying and make others feel as though the giver were angling for something—as if the giver "expected a receipt," lamented one writer. What makes a good compliment? These are the basics:

- *Be sincere:* Complimenting someone just because you think it's a good idea is a bad idea. Phoniness is easy to spot and destroys credibility. So if the luncheon speaker was a flop, don't gush about her speech. Talk about her effort, thank her for her time, and note her other accomplishments.
- *Be specific:* "That was a marvelous casserole" is better than "You're a terrific cook." "That sales research was right on target" is better than "Great job!"
- *Don't compare:* Never compare one person's accomplishment to another's.

In addition, compliments should be consistent with the setting and the relationship between giver and recipient.

THE WORKPLACE

So what about the boss's new haircut? If she or he is a longtime colleague and you're on very friendly terms, it's fine to compliment it. In most cases, however, it's best to stick to compliments on a colleague's work, rather than his or her appearance.

That goes double for remarks made to someone above or below you on the organizational chart. Because these relationships contain a power dynamic, personal remarks may unintentionally become highly loaded or easily misunderstood. So feel free to compliment your administrative assistant—but for his or her skills rather than appearance.

GETTING PERSONAL

An acquaintance looks far different from when you last met. Maybe she or he lost weight, or had a makeover or cosmetic surgery. You want to say something positive, but you're on delicate ground regarding the reason. So what do you say? Just, "You look absolutely marvelous!" with a big exclamation point in your voice. If the Marvelous Looking Person gives you a glimpse of the details, you can chat a bit about them. But if he or she merely thanks you, drop it and change the subject.

CARING FOR YOUR COMPLIMENT

This is how you respond to a compliment: *"Thank you."*

Some unacceptable alternatives include:

- "Are you nuts? I'm a *cow!*"
- "It was nothing."
- "Oh, you're not serious."
- "Please. I just threw this together."

And so forth. Never dispute, disparage, or diminish a compliment. To do so is to insult the giver by questioning his or her judgment, standards, taste, or—worst—sincerity. Much better to smile, savor the moment—and watch for the next chance to offer that great feeling to others!

*

24

NEGOTIATE

Donald Trump

✳

*Donald Trump is a real estate developer and owner of
properties, including the Taj Mahal casino and Trump
Plaza. He is also owner of the Miss Universe, Miss Teen
USA, and Miss USA beauty pageants. Trump is the
author of four books, including* The Art of the Deal.

NEGOTIATION is an art form. Some people, but not many,
are born with negotiation as an inherent talent. Most people need
to study and practice this art before becoming proficient. Here are
a few pointers:

1. Know exactly what you want, and focus on that.
2. View any conflict as an opportunity. This will expand your
   mind as well as your horizons.
3. Know that your negotiating partner/partners may well have
   exactly the same goals as you do. Do not underestimate them.

4. Patience is an enormous virtue and needs to be cultivated for successful negotiations on any level.

5. Realize that quiet persistence can go a long way. Being stubborn is often an attribute. The key is to know when to loosen up.

6. Remain optimistic at all times. Practice positive thinking—this will keep you focused while weeding out negative and detrimental people.

7. Let your guard down, but only on purpose. Watch how your negotiating partners respond.

8. Be open to change—it's another word for innovation.

9. Trust your instincts, even after you've honed your skills. They're there for a reason.

10. Negotiation is an art. Treat it like one.

*

25

LETITIA BALDRIGE

SHAKE HANDS

*

Letitia Baldrige was the social secretary to the White
House and chief of staff for Mrs. John F. Kennedy.
She is the author of twenty books, including
Letitia Baldrige's New Manners for New Times.

T H E handshake is usually the first physical contact adults have with one another, so for your own sake, make your handshakes a good experience. The other person will form several opinions of you in this process, such as whether you are a warm person; an affirmative, take-charge kind of person; a half-hearted, snobby person; or a wimpy, cold, hesitant, untrusting person.

A successful handshake depends upon how you execute it, when you do it, and where you do it. If you are young and inexperienced, or just feeling insecure, you will probably wonder if it is a wise move to extend your hand to shake someone else's. The answer is: *Do It!* Nine times out of ten it will make the other person notice you, feel kindly toward you, and consider you to be a person with good manners.

We all know that it is no fun to suffer through a rebuffed handshake. It's an out-and-out rejection, perhaps witnessed by many others. You stand there with your hand awkwardly extended, hanging in the air, and you would rather be walking the plank at that point than be where you are. But before you withdraw, red-faced with shame, think about it. Did you try to shake someone's hand while he or she was totally engaged in conversation with another person? Did you try to shake it when the rejector was standing in a receiving line, chatting with an illustrious neighbor? You may feel like a commoner at court, having committed an inexcusable faux pas, but it was probably just the circumstances at that particular moment that unfortunately caused your embarrassment. Common sense should tell you when *not* to be the initiator of a handshake.

When you first arrive at a gathering, seek out the host and introduce yourself with a handshake. When you are leaving, say goodbye and shake his or her hand again.

A good handshake carries some good body language with it. If you are the initiator of a handshake, step forward, put forth your right hand, and smile while looking the other person directly in the eyes. If you are meeting someone for the first time, add your voice: say your name distinctly.

Make sure your handshake is firm, not a limp-fish grip, but also not a killer body-builder crusher. Be sure not to have any remnants of the miniature pizzas, little hot dogs, or blue-cheese dip on your fingers.

And if your palms are eternally sweaty, take a quick, unobtrusive swipe on the seat of your pants or your skirt with your right hand, which will make the palm momentarily dry for the purpose of a handshake.

If you teach your kids at home how and when to shake hands, and reward them with praise when they do it right with guests, you're contributing to the socialization of America.

*

26

MAKE CONVERSATION

Morris L. Reid

*

*Morris L. Reid is the founder and managing director
of Westin Rinehart, an advisory and advocacy firm.
He began his career working for Secretary of
Commerce Ron Brown in the Clinton administration.*

CONVERSATION is a bit unappreciated in this age of sound
bites, e-mail, and enough television channels to keep all our eyes
glued and our mouths shut. Conversation should be important to
everyone as part of doing business, connecting with co-workers,
and even getting to know the neighbor. What follows are some
tips that I've found useful, whether speaking to a senator or a taxi-
cab driver.

DO YOUR HOMEWORK

What happened in school if you hadn't read the previous night's
assignment? You most likely had nothing to say. The same situation can happen in your adult life, and it could mean missing an
opportunity to make an important connection. Most people like to

think that what they do is important. If you can subtly and genuinely bring up an issue you find interesting about a person's company, line of work, or personal interest, they will be flattered, and you will have instantly made a connection. More important, you will be remembered for it. Even if some people are not talkative, they can certainly discuss that important project they've been working on.

A TWO-WAY STREET

Think of a conversation as a small relationship, with its ebbs and flows, and giving and taking. One-sided relationships usually don't work, and neither do one-sided conversations. Though you might have a wealth of things to say, don't translate that into excess verbiage. Keep in mind that you can learn something from almost everyone, and a basic human need is the feeling that what you have to say is worth hearing. Don't interrupt. Carefully listen to what others have to say, and ask thoughtful questions that signify you understand what they are talking about.

STAY ON TOP OF CURRENT EVENTS

By keeping your finger on the pulse of the world, you will know what people are thinking about, what matters, what's going to drive the future. Even if you haven't done your homework, you'll never be at a loss for words if you know what's going on in the world.

SHOW GOOD TASTE

It's easy, after a conversation begins to flow, to let down your guard and become too comfortable in the situation. This is risky. It is best to leave gossip, sarcasm, and complaining in general out of business conversation. You never know who knows whom, and once you've made a nasty remark, it can be difficult to win back your credibility.

FAMILIES DO MATTER

To some, families can be the most important aspect of life, and so it only follows that taking a genuine interest in, say, your colleague's daughter playing on the school softball team can add great value to a relationship. This could make him feel valued as a co-worker, and though you may not see eye to eye on work issues, having shown a human side will help mediate future disagreements.

YOU DON'T ALWAYS HAVE
TO BE THE SMARTEST PERSON IN THE ROOM

Take a look at politicians. They can read a book to elementary-school students, and then turn around and command a room of PhDs. How do they do this? Because good conversationalists accept they cannot possibly know everything there is to know. Once this is realized, the fear of sounding unintelligent no longer becomes an issue. Make an effort to listen, and project your strengths in other ways.

NOT EVERYONE WANTS TO TALK ABOUT BUSINESS

As a conversationalist, you need to be sensitive to the interests of others, and that may mean talking about last night's baseball game rather than the upcoming merger. Remember the analogy of a conversation being like a relationship—don't try to squeeze someone right away.

BE INCLUSIVE, NOT EXCLUSIVE

A good conversationalist will bring people together and find ways to include everyone in the conversation. Someone sitting quietly at a table will feel uncomfortable and will probably leave not having had a good time. Listen to the flow of the conversation, and use what you learned from having done your homework to raise a related topic that everyone can weigh in on.

ARE YOU TALKING TO ME, OR THE GUY OVER MY SHOULDER?

Eye contact is very important to effective conversation. It not only projects your own confidence but makes a person feel like he or she is the most important person in the room to you at that moment.

AND THE WINNER IS . . .

. . . the person at the party, in the boardroom, at the family reunion, or at the coffee shop who realizes that conversation is about understanding what others want, and about genuinely conveying what he or she needs.

27

REMEMBER NAMES

GARY SMALL

*

*Dr. Gary Small is the Parlow-Solomon Professor on
Aging at UCLA and author of* The Memory Bible: An
Innovative Strategy for Keeping Your Brain Young *and*
The Memory Prescription: Dr. Gary Small's 14-Day
Plan to Keep Your Brain and Body Young.

ALMOST everyone experiences some difficulty remembering
people's names—sometimes only seconds after being introduced.
The main reason for this name-memory challenge is that often we
are not fully paying attention—we are hearing, but not truly listening. Fortunately, for those of us who take solace in being "good
with faces," there are many easy-to-learn strategies to make
remembering names easy.

It is helpful to repeat the person's name during an initial conversation, or to comment on how the person reminds you of
someone else you know of the same name. If a person has a complicated or unfamiliar name, you might ask how to spell it. Some-

times just visualizing an image of the name spelled out will fix it into your memory. Using a person's name when saying goodbye will also help secure it into your memory bank.

Perhaps the most effective method for remembering names and faces uses three basic memory skills I call *Look, Snap, and Connect.* First, make sure you consciously listen and observe the name (*Look*). Then create a mental snapshot (*Snap*) of the name and the face. Finally, *Connect* the name snap with the face snap.

To create a visual *Snap* for the face, pick out a feature that may be easy to remember. Simply look at the person's face and search for the most distinguishing feature—for example, a small nose, large ears, unusual hair, or deep wrinkles. Often the first outstanding feature you notice is the easiest to recall later.

In creating a *Snap* for the name, note that all names can be placed into two groups: those that have a meaning and invoke a visual image, and those that don't. Names like Carpenter, Katz, House, Bishop, Siegel, White, or Silver all have a meaning and can readily bring to mind an image. After meeting Mrs. Siegel, think of a seagull.

Other names that have no immediate meaning may require additional mental effort to remember. However, the names or the syllables and sounds within them can be associated with a substitute name or sound that does have a meaning. By linking these substitute words together, you can create a visual image that works. Sometimes we can break a name into syllables that contain meanings, and then *link* them afterward. For example, the name George Waters could be remembered through an image of a *gorge* with a stream of *water* rushing into it. The word or syllable substitutes do not need to be exact. Jane Shirnberger could be a *chain* draped over a *shined* shoe that steps on a *burger*. I sometimes prefer seeing a famous person with the same name. So Jane Shirnberger becomes *Jayne* Mansfield wearing *shined* shoes and eating a *burger*.

In the final step, you *Connect* the name to the face by creating a mental image involving both your visual snapshots: the *Snap* for the distinguishing facial feature and the *Snap* for the name. For example, if Mrs. Beatty has prominent lips, an effective face snap for her might be her *lips,* and the name snap might be an image of Warren *Beatty*. *Connect* them by visualizing Warren Beatty kissing her on the lips (but don't tell Annette Bening about this).

The images and substitute words need not be perfect. The process of thinking up the images and making the connections will fix them into memory so you never have to forget a name and face again.

*

28

READ BODY LANGUAGE

STEVE COHEN

*

Steve Cohen is known as the Millionaires' Magician.
He presents his show "Chamber Magic" at New
York's legendary Waldorf Towers Hotel and performs
internationally for celebrities, tycoons, and aristocrats.
He is the author of the soon-to-be-published
book Just Like Magic.

In every minute of interaction with other people, you project up to 10,000 nonverbal signals. More than the words you use, your tone of voice and your facial and body expressions convey volumes of information. It is extremely useful to read people's body language so that you can see past what they are *saying* and learn what they are *thinking*. There is no magic to following these simple steps, just a little detective work that would make Sherlock Holmes proud.

CHECK SIZE OF PUPILS

When you walk into a dark room, your pupils naturally dilate (become larger) so that your eyes can gather more information and more light. They also dilate when you see something you like. Look at the pupils of the people you are speaking with. If their pupils are large, it is a sign of approval—they like what they see!

EYE CONTACT

When people speak their honest feelings, they are able to maintain a comfortable degree of eye contact with you. However, most people tend to look away—either with their entire head, or with the eyes only—when they are not speaking their genuine feelings. Watch for this telltale sign that what you are hearing is not the complete story.

WATCH FOR FAKE SMILES

A smile is normally recognized as a sign of happiness, affection, and honesty. However, it is also possible to be on the receiving end of a *forced smile*. If someone is smiling at you through clenched teeth, or in a tight-lipped manner, the person may be trying to deceive you. Remember: it takes longer for a genuine smile to fade than a forced smile.

LOOK UNDER THE TABLE

Watch for fidgety leg movements and nervous leg bouncing, both of which indicate that the person is in a negative state. If you notice that someone is sitting with legs crossed and one of them is bouncing on the other, this may be an indication that he or she is feeling anxious. Also look at the combination of leg activity with arm position. When people simultaneously bounce their legs and cross their arms, it usually indicates that they are closed off.

SPOT A LIAR

In addition to checking cues given off by the eyes (see above), you can determine whether someone is fibbing by watching for the following signals: excessive hand gesturing, playing with an object in the hands, scratching the body, or tightening the lips by sucking them inward. Another dead giveaway is stiff movements of the upper body. A liar often tries to keep his body still, and if his torso appears too rigid, he may be trying too hard to control his true feelings.

TELL IF HE OR SHE IS INTERESTED

One clue that a woman may silently give off to encourage men at a cocktail party is to repeatedly stroke the long stem of her cocktail glass. This action is performed completely subconsciously, and has obvious sexual connotations. The male equivalent of this gesture is for him to gently rub his finger around the rim of his glass as they casually converse. These signs are clear cues that the other person is interested in you, and that you may not be going home alone!

29

LISTEN

LARRY KING

*

Larry King is the host of Larry King Live *on CNN*
and author of How to Talk to Anyone, Anytime,
Anywhere: The Secrets of Good Communication.

PEOPLE think I make a living asking questions, which is true, but only half the story. The other half is listening to the answers. So many people in broadcasting, and indeed in life, love the sound of their own voice and don't listen to what the other person is saying. The key is to focus. The truest thing I've ever heard in my life, and I don't know whom to credit for this statement, is "I never learned anything when I was talking." Think about the truth in this statement. If you apply this to your everyday life, in all areas of your life—personal and professional—you will be much richer in the long run. The key is to pay attention.

If it sounds off-base, follow up. If you don't understand what you're listening to, simply say: "I don't understand. Can you explain it further?" There is nothing wrong with not knowing. It is wrong, however, not to admit that you don't know.

Sometimes it is hard to get someone to talk, but if you keep working at it, results can be produced. Here's a good case in point. I was interviewing an award-winning fighter pilot in Miami who had shot down eleven enemy planes in World War II. He was a guest on my show one night and everyone was excited to listen to a bona fide hero. I had one hour with him. My first question was why he enlisted in the air corps. His answer was "I liked it." No follow-up. I could immediately tell that not only was this fellow nervous, but it seemed impossible that I was going to be able to get him to speak for a whole hour. He was shaking so much that I immediately switched gears and asked him about fear. I asked, "If there was an enemy plane at the top of this station, would you take a plane to fight it?" He said, "Yes." I said I would be afraid and asked him what he was afraid of in terms of doing this interview. He said he didn't know who was listening.

I successfully switched topics to a discussion of fear. Within ten minutes, he was saying things like "We dove through the clouds . . . I could see the whites of their eyes . . ." In other words, I had moved him into a territory that was *his* territory and expression came out. So the tip here is to look for the person's comfort zone. For example, you might think being an accountant is boring. But the accountant doesn't feel that way about his own profession. So you might ask something like "What fascinates you about accounting?" In other words, let the subject know you are in interested in him or her.

To sum it up, a conversation requires two people. Sometimes more. Listen to what the other person is saying. You can thank me later.

30

IMPROVE YOUR VOCABULARY

RICHARD LEDERER

✳

*Dr. Richard Lederer is a language columnist and author of
many books about language and humor, including his
bestselling* Anguished English *series. He hosts "A Way
with Words" on public radio and frequently appears as a
guest on public and commercial radio shows. He has been
elected International Punster of the year and has been
awarded the Golden Gavel from Toastmasters International.*

JUSTICE Oliver Wendell Holmes once declared that "language is the skin of living thought." Holmes recognized that just as our skin bounds and encloses our body, so does our vocabulary bound and enclose our mental life. It's a matter of simple mathematics: the more words you know, the more choices you can make; the more choices you can make, the more accurate, vivid, and varied your speaking and writing will be.

Here are five methods you can use to enrich your vocabulary and, as a result, your ability to communicate:

1. READ! READ! READ!

When you were a child learning to speak, you seized each word as if it were a shiny toy. This is how you learned your language, and this is how you can expand your word stock. The best way to learn new words is through reading. Read for pleasure. Read for information. Read everything you can find on any subject that interests you—short stories, novels, nonfiction, newspapers, magazines. Soak up words like a sponge. The more words you read, the more words you will know.

2. INFER MEANING FROM CONTEXT

Detectives use clues to help them make deductions and solve cases. You can become a word detective and deduce the meaning of an unknown word by taking into account the words that surround it and the situation being talked or written about. Say you read the sentence "The advent of television swept away the huge, grandly ornate movie palaces of the 1920s and left in their place small, utterly functional faceless theaters." From context and the contrast to "utterly functional, faceless" you can infer that *ornate* means something like "elaborately decorated."

3. DIG DOWN TO THE ROOTS

Like people, words come in families. A word family is a cluster of words that are related because they contain the same root, a building block of language from which a variety of related words are formed. You can expand your vocabulary by digging down to the roots of an unfamiliar word and identifying the meanings of those roots.

Suppose that you encounter the word *antipathy* in speech or writing. From words like *antiwar* and *antifreeze* you can infer that the root *anti-*

means "against," and from words like *sympathy* and *apathy* that *path* is a root that means "feeling." From such insights it is but a short leap to deduce that *antipathy* means "feeling against something." This process of rooting out illustrates the old saying "It's hard by the yard but a cinch by the inch."

4. GET THE DICTIONARY HABIT

The practice of using the dictionary is essential in acquiring a mighty and versatile vocabulary. Keep an up-to-date dictionary by your side when you read. Whenever you run across a word that you are not sure of, look it up, a process that will probably take you no more than thirty seconds. Then record the word and its meaning on your private word list.

5. USE YOUR NEW WORDS

As soon as you have captured a new word in your mind, use it in conversation or writing. Try using at least one new word each day. Tell your parents how much you *venerate* them. Compliment your children on their *altruism* when they stoop to share the remote with you. Congratulate your business associates on their *edifying* presentation. Explain to Tabby that she shouldn't be so *intractable* about consuming her cat food.

And remind yourself not to *procrastinate* about acquiring and using new words. Make vocabulary growth a lifelong adventure. In the process, you will expand your thoughts and your feelings, your speaking, your reading, and your writing—everything that makes up you.

31

SPEED-READ

HOWARD STEPHEN BERG

*

Howard Stephen Berg is the world's fastest reader and principal of associatedlearning.com. Berg is the author of numerous books, including Speed-Reading the Easy Way.

T HE AVERAGE individual reads only about 200 words per minute. Yet you read the road in a car at speeds nearing 70 mph while simultaneously monitoring dashboard instruments, listening to the car radio, making cell calls, or carrying on conversations with passengers. All this is done effortlessly. So why do we read text so slowly when we read the road so quickly? The answer to this question holds the solution to higher reading speeds.

When reading the road, your eyes take in all the information as a movie. When you read a book, your brain converts the word-pictures into sound bites as a "little man" in the back of your head pronounces each word aloud. Reading is the only activity in which you use your eyes to hear, rather than see, information. We need a technique to make reading a more visual experience.

Using hand motions can quickly increase your reading speed by making your eyes view text more visually. Hand motions also help overcome several habits that can slow down reading speed—habits like visual regression or repeating interesting information. Visual regression occurs when the eyes continually go back to read words or phrases that have already been completed. It might sound like this in your brain when visual regression is acting out: The . . . The dog . . . The dog ate . . . The dog ate a bone. Interesting information is pleasurable, and your brain desires pleasure. If something you read was funny, or interesting, it is tempting to read it again to reexperience the pleasure. Unfortunately, this is done at the expense of your reading speed.

Visual regression—and the temptation of repeatedly reading the same information—can quickly be overcome by the proper use of the hands during reading. In an orchestra, the conductor uses his baton to coordinate all the musicians. While speed-reading, your hands perform the role of the conductor's baton. They move your eyes rapidly across the page. Here are two simple steps to begin increasing your reading speed by using hand motions:

1. Place your fingers at the start of a line, and quickly move them toward the right margin.
2. Make certain that your hand moves completely across the page from margin to margin.

There are three possible ways to coordinate your eye-hand action:

1. Your hand can lead your eyes across the line of text by moving in front of your focus.

2. Your hand can push your eyes across the line of text by staying behind your focal point.
3. Your hand can underline text with your eyes focusing directly above your hand.

Experiment to find the position that feels best for you.

Now that you can control your eye movements using your hand, you are ready to begin dramatically increasing your reading speed. Here's a simple 4-minute exercise:

1. Set a clock to beep after each minute.
2. Read for 1 minute at your peak comprehension rate.
3. Read at double your comprehension rate for 1 minute. You will not be able to comprehend text during this minute, but you will be making your brain work harder so it can read faster during the fourth minute.
4. Read at triple your comprehension rate for 1 minute. Again, you will not be able to comprehend text during this minute.
5. Read at your peak comprehension rate. Amazingly, you will be reading faster—and with comprehension!

*

32

MAKE AN EDUCATED GUESS

STANLEY H. KAPLAN

*

Stanley Kaplan is founder of Kaplan, Inc., a leading

test-preparation company.

THINK about how many educated—or not so educated— guesses you've made in real life. We constantly find ourselves making decisions based on limited information. The techniques I've developed for standardized tests are just as applicable to making educated guesses in real life. Following are some simple rules for making sound guesses.

RULE OUT OBVIOUS DISTRACTIONS

Part of making a good guess is ruling out obviously bad choices. Let's say you're trying to decide what to get your in-laws for their fortieth wedding anniversary. Without knowing much about their personal tastes and preferences, you can eliminate many choices. Rap concert tickets or a toaster are probably both bad ideas. If they're old enough to be celebrating their fortieth anniversary, they probably don't like popular music, and are likely to have already accumulated several toasters over the years that are now in storage. Eliminating the wrong choice is the first step on the way to deducing the right one.

OBSERVE CAREFULLY

You are at the airport and you run into an acquaintance, but you can't remember his name. Before you take a wild guess, look for clues. For example, a luggage tag on his bag may reveal his name, or at least his initials. Pay attention to the details, or you risk missing the tip-off.

LOOK FOR PATTERNS

The way things have gone in the past is often your best indication of how they will go in the future. If last Saturday night your favorite restaurant was packed because the movie theater crowd next door had just poured out, chances are this Saturday will be no different. Notice past patterns, and you're on your way to a smarter guess today.

USE OCCAM'S RAZOR: THE SIMPLEST EXPLANATION FOR A PHENOMENON IS USUALLY THE RIGHT ONE

It's late April and your business hears from the IRS that your tax forms and payment have not been received, yet you are certain that you sent them in. While you could entertain a scenario in which your business competitor intercepts your mail as a means of getting you in trouble for failing to pay your taxes on time, it's a lot more likely that the post office or the IRS lost or misplaced your mail. When in doubt, don't fall for the fancy, convoluted answer. Simpler is usually right.

USE WHAT YOU KNOW

You usually know more than you think. Even the most basic facts will take you far. If it is April and you're in a college town seeking a quiet place to meet a friend for a drink, it's clear you're better off trying a bar far from campus than the one across the street from the main gates. Remembering that universities empty out over the summer will help you know that when June hits, your best bet is now a place close to campus. "Common knowledge" can take you uncommonly far.

Complete certainty is a rare luxury in life. We are usually guessing, and an educated guess is the best we can do.

*

33

TELL A STORY

IRA GLASS

*

Ira Glass is host and producer of Public Radio International's This American Life.

START your story with a provocative piece of bait. This can be a big original thought about the action that's to come, like: "Happy families are all alike; every unhappy family is unhappy in its own way." That's the sort of thing you might invent if you were one of the greatest writers who ever lived. If you're more like me, simply reach for an original, snappy-sounding idea that might more or less be true: "Society has a deal with people in certain unpleasant jobs." Or: "Like you, I'm tired of the Internet."

The other way to begin a story, the easier way, is simply to get the action rolling: "We were somewhere around Barstow on the edge of the desert when the drugs began to take hold." "Last night I dreamt I went to Rome again." "Marley was dead to begin with." Classics. You just start things in motion, let one event lead to the next.

Remember, at its heart, a story is simply a sequence of actions. *This* thing happened, and then *this,* and that led to *this.* If you do it right, the sheer momentum will keep people engaged, because it'll feel like it's all leading *somewhere.* Also, handily, a sequence of actions, laid out this way, will generally raise questions ("What happened in Rome?" "Who's Marley?"), and unanswered questions are more bait, pulling people deeper into your story.

Be specific in the details. The surprising, telling detail is part of the pleasure of a story. In his account of attending a summer camp for American kids in Greece, David Sedaris explains that they'd go to gift shops and shoplift "pint-sized vases, little pom-pommed shoes, and coffee mugs reading SPARTA IS FOR A LOVER." In any piece of writing, the more you're in it to amuse yourself, the better it'll be. Work in stuff you find funny, or moving, or interesting. If you never find things funny, moving, or interesting, please don't try to create stories.

Part of the craft of telling a story well is sensing when you should keep the action going, and when you can pause for description, or some little observation you make, or an interesting digression. In many kinds of stories, you'll want to stop the action for a moment of reflection about what the point of the story is. It can be a character in the story who does this introspecting, or it can be you, the narrator.

In most stories, we watch someone go through some experience, and it leads to some new perspective about the world—usually for them, but sometimes only for us. Sometimes this new perspective is stated straight out. Sometimes we observe the characters' transformation though their actions. They get into situations we've seen them in before, but now they act differently. If no one in your story changes and no one learns anything, *Seinfeld* notwithstanding, it's probably not a story.

That's it for the basic building blocks. Then it all comes down to taste. It's impossible to overstate how much of this is about your taste, in the details you choose, the things you notice about people, the conclusions you come to. That's what makes the difference between something great and something that's just okay.

Finally: your story should be surprising and lead to some surprising new thought about the world. When a story sucks, it's usually because it doesn't feel new. Or because it feels fake. Or because it's not about something worth talking about in the first place. Avoid that.

*

34

CONDUCT A BACKGROUND INVESTIGATION

Terry Lenzner

*

Terry Lenzner is the chairman of The Investigative
Group International. He was the assistant chief
counsel to the Senate Watergate Committee, serving
the first congressional subpoena on a U.S. President.

S CENARIO: You need information on a person you, a close relative, or a friend is considering marrying. Or you are negotiating a transaction and need to know the background, reputation, and honesty of the individual(s).

SOLUTION: Research through the following steps.

1. FIRST STOP: THE WEB

The Internet is the fastest and least expensive way of obtaining personal data, starting with the search engine Google. You can "google" someone by entering a name, and Google will deliver several listings directly related to the name. If the name is a common one, you may have to associate it with additional details, such as a date of birth or geographical location.

2. ASK QUESTIONS

Don't be shy about asking people for details regarding the subject's education and employment, birth date and location, and military service. These inquiries can be done subtly by inserting into conversations questions pertaining to these personal facts. This route of questioning requires you to be patient and reasonably persistent. Remember, a good investigator is a good listener.

3. BACK TO SCHOOL

Educational history can be a great source for additional information on a person. For example, alumni magazines often provide personal, professional, and other relevant information. School magazines and yearbooks are also a great way to locate a subject's classmates, teammates, and roommates, all of whom might have additional insights on the person.

4. THE PROFESSIONAL

If a life-changing or business decision is dependent on your search, you may consider hiring a respected professional investigative firm. A licensed investigator is able to legally access more than one hundred databases available only by subscription. These databases provide a wide array of facts on individuals, including a lifetime of addresses; lists of neighbors, liens, bankruptcies, judgments, press reports, lawsuits, regulatory actions, convictions, and owned property, including automobiles and boats; and employment listings for every job a person has ever held.

5. THE INTERVIEW

Facts determined from your investigation are not always black and white, but often gray and less easily defined, making it more difficult to decide a course of action. The individuals identified by your investigator or through your initial search can help you answer some of the unanswered questions. But first you must find out as much as possible about the interviewee's personal and professional history and relationship to the subject. You don't want the interviewee's prejudices or ulterior motives to twist or shade the facts you need to help you determine a course of action.

6. ADDITIONAL SOURCES

Before closing the interview, you or your investigator should inquire whether the interviewee can provide additional sources who might have relevant information, as well as their addresses and relevancy to your inquiry. You should also ask if there are any other questions the interviewee should answer to complete the picture.

7. THE SUCCESSFUL INTERVIEWER

Be a patient listener with a sense of curiosity. In the interview process, you will acquire the instincts that will help you to translate body language and to identify and squelch attempts to obfuscate the truth. During the Watergate investigation of 1973, I developed sensitivity to body language, facial expressions, and speech rhythms that has since helped me navigate through questioning that often leads to an admission of improper and often illegal activity.

35

DELIVER BAD NEWS

Dr. Robert Buckman

*

Robert Buckman, MD, PhD, is a medical oncologist at the Princess Margaret Hospital and a professor in the Department of Medicine at the University of Toronto. He is also an adjunct professor at the M. D. Anderson Cancer Center, University of Texas. He has written fourteen books, including I Don't Know What to Say *and* How to Break Bad News: A Guide for Health Care Professionals.

B REAKING bad news to people is almost always a difficult, awkward, and painful experience—for the person who breaks the news as well as for the recipient. As a physician specializing in oncology (cancer treatment), I've had to break bad news frequently. Along with a colleague, I have developed a strategy called SPINES to make it easier and more effective.

The secret to breaking bad news is not what you say, but how you *listen* and how you *respond* to the other person. The six steps of the SPINES strategy consist of the Setting (S), Perception

(P), Initiating (I), Narrative (N), Emotions (E), and Strategy & Summary (S).

The first step is to make the physical *Setting* as comfortable as possible. Sit down and create an air of privacy (shut the door, turn off the television, etc.). Next, do your best to ascertain what the other person is feeling or suspecting—assess their *Perception* of the situation. Are they worried? Do they already think something bad has happened? Or is this going to come out of the blue?

How you assess the situation will help you in the next step—*Initiation*. The exact words you use will depend on your own personal style and on your relationship with the other person. If the news you will be delivering is unexpected, you might use phrases such as "I'm afraid I have to tell you something about . . ." or, "I've just been called by the hospital: there's been an accident and . . . ," or, "I've been talking to the doctor about . . ."

The next two steps of the strategy must occur simultaneously: you give the other person a *Narrative* of what has happened, and you respond to their reactions and *Emotions* as you do so. The *Narrative* is the story of what has happened. As you explain the events, you need to address and acknowledge *Emotions*—in many respects, this is the most important process in the communication. If you are able to respond well to the other person's emotions, you will be a good and effective communicator, even if the other steps and processes are not perfect.

The most practical and valuable way of addressing and acknowledging emotions is a technique called the *empathic response*—and it consists of three steps:

1. You *identify the emotion* that has arisen—whether it is shock, disbelief, anger, fear, distress, or a mixture of any of these and others.
2. You *identify the cause or source of the emotion*—in this situation it is almost always the actual news itself.
3. You respond in a way that shows you have made the *connection* between steps 1 and 2.

For example, if you are bearing news of an accident or even a death, an empathic response might be as simple as "This is clearly a terrible shock." You can add an expression of sympathy: "This is a terrible shock—I'm so sorry for you." But the important part is to start with a clear empathic response—demonstrating that you have recognized and acknowledged the other person's emotion.

The final step is to make a *Strategy* to explain what you are prepared to do. Make a plan that is realistic and reasonable, including a clear offer of what's going to happen next and when you will next check in with the other person. It doesn't matter if what you offer is modest—what matters is that you fulfill your promise!

By using the SPINES strategy, you can do a great deal to support others at difficult times.

*

36

APOLOGIZE

BEVERLY ENGEL

＊

Beverly Engel is a psychotherapist and author of fifteen self-help books, including The Power of Apology: Healing Steps to Transform All Your Relationships, *which was a finalist for the Books for a Better Life Award.*

APOLOGIZING involves more than merely saying the words "I'm sorry." When we apologize, we acknowledge to the other person that we have done something that was hurtful or is potentially hurtful to them. We are admitting to them and to ourselves that we made a mistake. Therein lies the rub.

Even though most of us feel better when we apologize, there is an equally powerful opposing drive within each of us to protect our ego, our pride, and our carefully constructed and defended public self. We hesitate to apologize because to do so is to admit we are flawed and fallible. To apologize is to set aside our pride long enough to admit our imperfections.

At times, it is the fear of consequences that keeps people from apologizing. Many people fear that if they take the risk of apologizing, they may be rejected. Others fear that by apologizing they risk being exposed, losing respect, or having their reputation ruined. And some people fear retaliation. It is precisely because making an apology can be a risk that makes it all the more meaningful. Apology is an important social ritual that takes courage, humility, and finesse.

My formula for communicating and making a meaningful apology involves the three Rs: regret, responsibility, and remedy.

REGRET

In order for the recipient to take you seriously, you need to convey an expression of regret for having caused the inconvenience, hurt, or damage. This includes an expression of empathy toward the other person—an acknowledgment that you understand how your action (or inaction) must have felt to him or her. Having empathy toward the recipient is the most important part of your apology. When you truly have empathy, the recipient will feel it. Your apology will wash over him or her like a healing balm.

RESPONSIBILITY

You also need to convey an acceptance of responsibility for your actions. This means that you should refrain from blaming anyone else for what you did and avoid making excuses for your actions. Instead, accept full responsibility for what you did and for the consequences of your actions.

REMEDY

Finally, you need to include a statement of your willingness to take action to remedy the situation. This could include promising not to repeat your action, or committing to work toward not making the same mistake again, or making restitution for any damages you may have caused.

The two most important underlying aspects of an apology are your intention and your attitude. Your apology will only feel believable to the recipient—and your attempt to rehabilitate yourself will only succeed—if your apology comes from a sincere attempt to express heartfelt feelings of regret, and if you take responsibility for your actions.

∗

37

SPEAK IN PUBLIC

JAMES WAGSTAFFE

*

James Wagstaffe is a First Amendment attorney and a professor at Stanford University, where he teaches practical speech communication. He is the author of Romancing the Room: How to Engage Your Audience, Court Your Crowd, and Speak Successfully in Public. *Wagstaffe was National Collegiate Speaking Champion while a student at Stanford. He is a regular columnist for the* Los Angeles Daily Journal *and the* San Francisco Daily Journal.

T H E R E are some universal truths that allow you to distinguish communications that *soar* from those that *bore*. Communicators who desire to romance the room should come to view these truths as *imperatives.*

1. ROMANCING MEANS NEVER HAVING TO SAY YOU ARE SORRY

We often apologize in advance while downselling our communication skills. Don't do it. Communicators reveal a lack of confidence in themselves and their messages when they make such apologies. Apologetic communicators may harbor a fear of failure or embarrassment, so they ensure they'll be the first to give themselves the expected poor "grade." Just before someone opens your gift, this is similar to saying, "The receipt is in the package. If you don't like the present, please feel free to return it." Show confidence in gift choices and presentations. *Caveat:* An apology *is* in order if you have inadvertently caused harm (e.g., an unintended slight) or not completed some promise (e.g., you show up late).

2. BEGIN ROMANCING LIKE A BLIND DATE

The *first 30 seconds* of any encounter are vitally important. Anybody who's been on a blind date knows the pressure of the initial greeting. Likewise, thinking about and then making a positive first impression are imperative if we want to romance packed rooms with success:

- *Look in a mirror!* Is your hair out of place? Have your stockings run? Maybe there's something caught in your teeth.
- *Begin with a bang!* First impressions are often easy to read: if the listeners laugh, roar with approval, or seem physically and mentally engaged, you've got them.
- *Answer the why of "Why should they listen to you?"* Once you have their attention, give the audience a reason to keep listening by letting them know your speaking objectives.

3. ROMANCE THE FLY—LOOK THEM IN THE EYE

A friend of mine can "romance a fly." Here's how he does it: He's in a room with a fly buzzing all about. He stands very still, makes eye contact with the fly, and virtually mesmerizes the insect. It lands, stops buzzing, and my friend approaches *slowly* with an open hand. He then gently closes his hand to capture the fly and transport it outdoors.

You must romance the audience like a fly. Communicators must look their listeners in the eye, make Zen-like contact, and capture the listeners' attention with directness. The listeners will stop "buzzing" around physically and mentally, now paying rapt attention to your message. Make friendly, engaging contact with as many people as reasonably possible.

4. ADD SPICE TO YOUR ROMANCING THROUGH VARIETY

The absolute nemesis to successful romancing is boredom. To combat potential monotony (and loss of attention), you must offer variety to keep the "romance" in the relationship. This means varied vocal patterns and supporting materials as examples. Such variety will produce a kaleidoscope of reactions. Spice it up and keep your listeners leaning in to catch your every word.

5. END BEFORE EXPECTED: THE PREMATURE EVACUATION

Final impressions are very important. Certainly, you want to guarantee they don't stop listening before you stop talking! To increase your odds of success at achieving a romancing communication, you must engage in a "premature evacuation"—*end before they expect you to end . . . always!*

- *Know time expectations:* Listeners have preexisting expectations as to the length of your presentation. End your talk
  short of this anticipated length. Excess length can cost you a
  favorable review, a large penalty for going overtime. No matter how solid your presentation has been, the listeners will
  get the feeling that it is going on too long.
- *Be ever aware of listeners' attention span:* The bottom line is
  that you must constantly be aware of your listeners' attention
  span. Don't overstay your welcome, and you'll keep the
  romance alive throughout your communication.

*

HOME
LIFE

38

BALANCE YOUR CHECKBOOK

TERRY SAVAGE

*

Terry Savage is the Chicago Sun-Times
personal finance columnist and author of
The Savage Truth on Money.

$\mathbf{B}$ALANCING your checkbook is like balancing your life. You don't have to do it. But once you get your money—or your life— under control, you have a much better chance of getting what you want. The whole idea of balancing your checkbook is to make sure that your records and the bank's records agree, and to keep track of what you do with your money—and how much you have.

Today, almost every bank or financial institution offers online bill payments. But if you're determined to stick to paper checking, be sure to write down every check, subtract to get a current balance, and then compare with your bank statement. This is the drudge work of money management.

Sort those paper checks by number, then make a mark in your checkbook to show that each one has "cleared" (been paid) by the bank. If there are any missing checks—those you've written but that haven't been deposited by the payee—you'll have to subtract them from the balance on your statement. One day they'll come through, and you don't want to be surprised with overdraft fees because you forgot to have money in your account to cover them.

Now, aren't you ready for a better system? You'll be surprised how much time, money, and mental aggravation you can save by paying your bills online at your bank's website. It's easy, it's safe—and you never get late fees. Plus, the bank creates and balances your checkbook for you.

Here's how it works. Just go to your financial institution's website. There's sure to be a spot to click for information and to sign up to online bill pay. Once you create a password, you'll be entering the highly secured world of the bank transfer system, where trillions of dollars are moved every day. They won't lose track of you. And no one can withdraw money from your checking account. Guaranteed. And if you're worried about being lost in cyberspace, each bank has a toll-free number with trained representatives to guide you through the process of getting started.

Just take your stack of bills to be paid, and the first time through you'll have to enter the payee's name and address, as well as your account number with that merchant. You can pay big companies, like your credit card, electric bill, telephone bill, or mortgage. But you can also pay *anyone*—including the money you owe your sister, or the service that mows your lawn. If they aren't set up to receive money electronically, the bank will actually print a paper check and send it to them.

After you go through the setup process the first time you pay a bill, the bank computer will remember your payees' names, addresses, and your account numbers. The next time, all you have to do is click on the name and pay the current amount due from the bills as you receive them.

Here's the best part. The bank will create your own online check register. And subtract. And balance your checkbook, letting you see which checks have cleared, and which are still outstanding. Just go to the bank's website anytime and you'll get all the current information. It's like being able to peek over the bank counter and see the teller's screen!

Having an instant update on your cash flow is a key ingredient in maintaining control of your personal finances—and in reaching your financial goals.

*

39

SAVE MONEY

Suze Orman

*

Suze Orman is the author of numerous books,
including The Laws of Money, The Lessons of Life.
She is the personal finance editor on CNBC and host
of CNBC's The Suze Orman Show. *Orman is also a*
contributing editor to O: The Oprah Magazine.

THERE'S really no mystery to this, my friends. The best way to save money is to not spend money. But I know that's not as easy as it sounds. Getting into a saving routine is a lot like going to the gym—we know that exercising is good for us, yet it is hard to commit to a regular workout schedule.

I'll leave the workout challenge to another expert and focus on giving you a game plan so that you can become a savvy saver. Saving is best done little by little. As I like to say, "Fortunes are made zero by zero." If you commit to my plan and stick with it, you will become an accomplished—and wealthy—saver.

Here's the secret: from this day forward, never spend your change. We're going to make you a successful saver one penny at a time. Perhaps that sounds rather low-tech to you, but trust me, it is incredibly effective. Let's say you walk into the corner store and purchase a magazine for $4.25 by handing the cashier a $5 bill. I want you to take the 75 cents in change and deposit it in your savings stash. Literally create a place in your wallet or purse for your Change. (A good old piggy bank will work just fine.)

Before you start rolling your eyes at this simple process, try it out. I've had plenty of folks give my change strategy the test, and on average the monthly savings is between $30 and $60. I know that doesn't seem like you're on the road to riches. But your next job is to take your monthly change savings and invest it, preferably in a tax-deferred retirement account such as a Roth IRA. Assuming you have at least a 10-year time horizon, I recommend a low-cost index mutual fund such as Vanguard Total Stock Market fund. Over the long term—we're talking decades, not months—U.S. stocks have averaged about a 10 percent annualized gain. If you can invest just $50 a month using my change strategy, your account would grow to $113,024 in 30 years, assuming a 10 percent average return. If you keep at it for 40 years, the account would be worth $316,204. Not bad, eh?

And if you can commit to an even more aggressive strategy, your savings will be even greater. See if you can save all your single dollar bills. I bet you would have at least $75 a month in single bills. Invest those George Washingtons at a 10 percent return and you will have $474,306 in 40 years. You can make nearly half a million dollars just by stashing away your spare change! That's my two cents on the subject.

40

UNDERSTAND YOUR PET

WARREN ECKSTEIN

*

*Warren Eckstein is the contributing Pet and Animal
Editor for NBC's* Today. *He is the former animal
expert on* Live with Regis and Kathie Lee. *He
is the author of eleven books including*
How to Get Your Cat to Do What You Want *and*
How to Get Your Dog to Do What You Want.

D ECADES ago, pets spent most of their time outdoors. More
often than not, the family pet was named King, Princess, Duke,
Fluffy, or Snookums. Today, it's not uncommon for the family pet
to be named Bob, Harry, Sally, Tiffany, or Suzy. This humaniza-
tion of the family pet reflects a major change in the way people
view their furry companions. No longer are pets considered
merely animals—our pets are now beloved members of the family. In fact, today, more likely than not, these four-footed family
members live inside the home and in the majority of homes
even sleep in the family bed. Even the term "pet owner" has been

changed to "pet guardian" in several U.S. cities, to reflect our pets' upgraded status.

Because we have taken pets into our human environment, we can no longer treat them merely as animals and expect them to respond as humans. Instead, we must learn to integrate them into our lives and help them become part of our human lifestyle. For example, include your pets in conversations, activities, and outings. Let them be part of the decision-making process in vacation planning, even types of exercise. If you treat your pet with love and respect, your pet will respond in positive, astonishing ways.

Pets, just like people, have a curious way of living up or down to the image you project for them. Give your pets high expectations considering their own abilities, and they'll reach for the stars trying to please you. Conversely, by constantly telling them how displeased you are with their behavior, or micro-managing them into your idea of perfection, you'll rip apart their self-esteem, making it impossible for them to believe in you and, most of all, in themselves.

The best way to create a confident pet, and a pet that behaves well, is to spend more time focusing on the things the pet does right than those the pet does wrong. It's important to present a clear picture for your pet of exactly what makes you happy. We all know that pets are willing to please their owners—so when they make mistakes, don't you think it might be that their owners are sending the wrong signals?

Here's where family continuity is critical. Take, for example, the call to my national radio show in which the woman expressed her discontent with her dog's jumping on the couch. On the extension, the husband is telling me how he enjoys having the dog next to him on the couch. I'm waiting for an e-mail from the dog saying, "Hey, Warren, isn't this the definition of neurosis?"

Or take the woman whose cat constantly bothers her while she's on the phone. Think about it—there's no one else in the house, the woman's obliviously talking away . . . Who does the cat think the woman is talking to?

Understand that pets have emotions and need coping systems to deal with new situations like a new baby, a grandparent moving in, kids going to college, and especially divorce.

What you put into your pet is what you get out of your pet. The two most important factors are the environment and how the family members relate to the pet. In other words, your family plays a tremendous role in influencing your pet's personality, intelligence, and disposition. So don't forget to give your pet a hug and a kiss!

*

CARE FOR A HOUSEPLANT

JACK KRAMER

*

Jack Kramer is an expert on plants
and the author of numerous books, including
Easy-Care Guide to Houseplants.

TODAY, houseplants are as much a part of the home as furniture. And while there are many different methods to grow plants, there are only a few rules to follow to make them healthy.

BASIC REQUIREMENTS

Plants require water, light, feeding, suitable temperatures, and, above all, observation. Don't fuss with your plants, but rather give them some tender loving care. Plants will indicate whether they are happy. Healthy plants have fresh green leaves of good texture, erect stems, and, in general, a robust appearance. Drooping leaves and straggly stems indicate a plant that is not happy in its environment.

SELECTION

With so many plants available, it is important you select those that will respond to your home environment. Buy plants that are appropriate for the environment you can give them rather than adjusting your home condition to the plants. Here is a list of amenable houseplants that will adapt to home temperatures of, say, 58 to 80 degrees Fahrenheit:

- *Aroids:* Aglaonema, Alocasia, Anthurium, Dieffenbachia, Philodendrons, Scindapsus, Syngoniums
- *Bromeliads:* Aechmea, Guzmania, Neoregelia, Nidularium, Tillandsia
- *Ferns:* Adiantum, Areca, Caryota, Cyrtomium, Rhapis
- *Orchids*—Cattleya, Dendrobiums. Epidendrums, Oncidium, Phalaenopsis

SOIL

Most people worry over the proper soil for plants. Forget it. Almost any ordinary packaged soil will do fine for most houseplants. Be sure the soil is moist, smells like the good earth, and feels grainy like a baked potato. It should also be porous so water can soak through and not accumulate on the top of the soil.

CONTAINERS

Practically any container is suitable for a plant, but basically the old-fashioned unglazed terra cotta pot is the best because the color goes with most home decors, and unglazed terra cotta allows slow evaporation of water from the side of the pot, so the plant never really becomes soggy.

POTTING

When you get your plant home from the nursery or market, repot it. The medium it is grown in may not be proper soil. Replace the "filler" or lightweight material with good mealy soil as outlined above.

FEEDING

Forget about specific plant foods. A general houseplant fertilizer is fine for all plants. Just be sure to follow the package directions.

WATERING

Do not overwater plants. Without optimum conditions, plants cannot tolerate gallons of water. Keep the soil evenly moist. To test the dampness of soil, insert your finger one inch into the medium. If it feels moist, do not water. However, do not allow soil to become overly dry, which creates a caked soil that water cannot penetrate. Most plants should be watered a few times a week in spring and summer and once a week in fall and winter.

LIGHT

Contrary to popular opinion, most plants do not want direct sunlight because it can burn foliage; plants like filtered or scattered light. So an area near windows protected by a screen is a good place for the green scene.

INSECTS

Years ago, insects were a common worry, but this is not so today. Most plants are generally free of pests. Occasionally a mealybug, white spider, or thrips will attack unhealthy plants. Buy a general houseplant insecticide and use it sparingly. Do not purchase high-powered insect sprays containing unwanted chemicals. Some organic remedies: alcohol on a cloth will eliminate aphids; ashes will get rid of mealybugs.

HINTS FOR SUCCESS

1. Trim and groom plants every month or so. Remove dead leaves and stems and cut off stray growth.
2. If a plant does not do well in one place, move it a few feet away.
3. Keep leaves shiny and clean by washing with a damp cloth. Do not use leaf-shining preparations, which can clog leaf pores and create problems for the plant.
4. Avoid plant-watering devices that release water slowly; these come in various forms. Water your plants yourself so you can observe how they are growing. Also, watering and nurturing the plant is good therapy for you. It keeps you involved with the green scene and the world.
5. Slow down, enjoy your plants, and be proud of growing healthy beautiful plants. I have done it for thirty-five years and still enjoy tending to my own indoor garden without any artificial help from concoctions and preparations.

Plants are natural living things and want to survive. They will with a little common sense and some care.

42

PREPARE FOR A DISASTER

Marsha J. Evans

*

*Marsha Evans is president and CEO of the
American Red Cross and retired from the
U.S. Navy as a rear admiral.*

WHETHER you're worried about a tornado or a terrorist attack,
taking these simple but important steps can help keep you safer:

1. Know which kinds of natural and human-caused disasters
   pose a risk for your area. Don't forget home fires—the most
   common disaster of all!
2. Discuss with your family the types of disaster that could
   occur and what actions are necessary to prepare and respond.
3. Pick two places for the family to meet, one near your home in
   case you need to evacuate, and one outside your neighborhood
   in case you cannot return home. Choose an out-of-town
   "family contact" person family members will call to report how
   they are doing. Long-distance phone lines often work even
   when local phone lines are jammed. Have everyone memorize
   meeting places and your family contact's phone numbers.

4. Identify at least two ways out of each room in your home. It's very important to practice evacuating. Every year, families survive a fire because their children remembered their evacuation drill.

5. Ask for emergency plans from every family member's school or workplace and discuss them.

6. Put together basic supplies you will need if you must evacuate or have to remain in your home ("shelter in place"). Pack these in something you can carry, like a duffel bag. The goal is to have everything you need to survive for three days without electricity or water. Some key items:

   • For each person, include 3 days' food that won't spoil or need to be heated; 3 gallons of water; bedding; and a change of clothes.

   • For each person, also put in any special items they can't do without, such as baby diapers and formula, essential medicines, spare eyeglasses, etc. If you have children, include a deck of cards, small travel games, puzzles, books, etc., to help time pass.

   • Include a flashlight and battery-powered radio with extra batteries; first aid supplies; a manual can opener; plates, cups, and utensils; and copies of essential documents.

   • Additional items to consider are basic tools (including a wrench to turn off utilities), tape, sewing kit, plastic sheeting, a small fire extinguisher, a map, and cleanup supplies for you and your home.

7. Learn how and when to turn off gas, electricity, water, and other utilities. Keep necessary tools near gas and water valves.

8. Learn how to keep yourself and your family safer by taking first aid, CPR, and disaster training classes.

43

SHOVEL SNOW

Mayor Anthony M. Masiello

*

*Anthony M. Masiello is mayor of Buffalo, New York,
one of the snowiest towns in America and four-time
contender for the Super Bowl.*

NOT ALL snow is created equal! Snow comes in a variety of consistencies:

- *Fluffy light:* Think *It's a Wonderful Life* or "I'm
  Dreaming of a White Christmas." Biggest advantage:
  easy to remove from sidewalks, driveways, and car
  windshields.
- *Regular:* Think any snow-tire commercial, *Grumpy Old
  Men,* or any ski-patrol movie. Can be difficult to
  remove from sidewalks, driveways, and car
  windshields.
- *Heavy wet:* Think slushed-ice confections. Biggest
  advantage of this type of snow is that it is "good packing"
  for snowballs and snowmen.

- *Frozen solid:* Think penguin exhibit at zoo. This is its own category and will not be discussed with the other types of snow.

THE GAME PLAN

THE EXHIBITION GAME

- 1 to 6 inches of fluffy light
- 1 to 4 inches of regular
- 1 to 3 inches of heavy wet

Anyone can handle this simple task. Very nice family activity, but you won't mind doing this job by yourself either. Dress warmly. Use any regular snow shovel. Grandma's hot cocoa is the traditional "warm me up" after completing the task.

THE REGULAR-SEASON GAME

- 6 to 12 inches of fluffy light
- 4 to 9 inches of regular
- 3 to 5 inches of heavy wet

This requires getting others involved. Dress warmly. Use a snow shovel with a steel-reinforced blade, which will be needed to scrape off the packed snow. Hot cider or other hot liquid is suggested.

THE PLAYOFF GAME

- 12 to 18 inches of fluffy light
- 9 to 15 inches of regular
- 5 to 9 inches of heavy wet

You need help! If you are married, your spouse must be out there with you. Likewise, if you have kids, they probably have the day off from school, so enlist their help too. Dress warmly, but you are going to sweat from this hard work. Your first layer of clothing should be cotton. Regular snow shovels with steel-reinforced blades are useful, but old-fashioned coal shovels are ideal in this situation because they are easier to handle. After working on this job, something stronger than hot chocolate may be appropriate.

THE SUPER BOWL

- 18 inches or more of fluffy light
- 15 inches or more of regular
- 9 inches or more of heavy wet

Hope your neighbor has a snow blower and he is a Good Samaritan. If not, round up all of the other neighbors' kids! This may cost you a few bucks.

THE APOCALYPSE

- 7 feet of any kind of snow

Call the governor to send the National Guard, call Congress for FEMA aid, and wait until spring!

FROZEN SOLID SNOW

This category requires extra equipment and probably extra people power. If it is above 20 degrees Fahrenheit outside, a healthy dose of rock salt must be spread evenly on the affected area. Other types of ice-melting substances such as calcium chloride must be used for severe temperatures. After ice begins to melt, you will need an ice pick or ice scraper to chop the ice into small chunks. Remove them with a regular snow shovel or with a coal shovel.

OTHER HELPFUL HINTS

- Shoveling is like voting. Do it early and often.
- Shovel snow into piles that will melt away from your sidewalk.
- Don't overdo it. Take your time and shovel in spurts if necessary.
- Kleenex or handkerchiefs are a must. Noses tend to run while shoveling snow.
- Make sure you remember the neighbor with the snow blower at Christmas time.

Let's get real. The average middle-aged body is not built for shoveling snow. Neither is mine. Whenever possible, leave it to the experts—the kids who are supple, flexible, and naive enough to think shoveling is worth the paltry sum you will pay them.

*

44

REMOVE A STAIN

LINDA COBB

✳

Linda Cobb, aka the Queen of Clean®, is the author
of six books, including Talking Dirty with the Queen
of Clean, *and has been featured on over one hundred*
talk shows with her stain-removal solutions. She is the
star of her own television series, Talking Dirty with
the Queen of Clean®, *on the DIY Network.*

To STAIN is human, to remove it divine. How to remove it can be a mystery. Prompt and proper treatment is the best way to keep a spot from becoming a stain. Here are some guidelines to turn you into a spot-solving guru.

- Always test any spot remover on a hidden area of the fabric before proceeding.
- Work on the stain from the wrong side of the fabric. This keeps you from pushing the spot into the fabric instead of out of it.

- Put a pad of paper toweling under the spot to help blot the stain as you work.
- Always blot. Never rub the spot.
- Remember to consider the type of fabric you are working on when selecting a spotting product. Delicate fabric requires a much gentler approach.
- Catching the spot while it is fresh will make your chances of successful removal almost 100 percent. Even blotting with cold water will give you time to react with the proper spotter.
- Never apply heat or put a garment in the dryer until you are sure the spot is removed.

You have a cleaning and spotting arsenal in your cupboards. There are many products lurking there that make great laundry spotters:

- *Alcohol:* Great for grass stains and so much more.
- *Ammonia:* Fights perspiration stains.
- *Baking soda:* Removes odors. Try adding ¼ cup to a bucket of warm water and drop in those smelly sports socks. Soak them for an hour and then pour bucket and all into the washer and launder as usual.
- *Club soda:* This is the "Oh my gosh, I can't believe I spilled that" spotter. Use on any fabric or surface that can be treated with water. A slight dabbing on dry-clean-only fabrics is also permissible—just be sure to test first! Use club soda on any spill: dab it on and blot it off. Club soda will keep spots from becoming stains.

- *Denture-cleaning tablets:* The cure-all for white table linens with food stains and white cotton with stains. Dissolve one tablet per ½ cup of warm water. Pour directly on the spot and let it sit 30 minutes or so, and then launder as usual.

- *Hydrogen peroxide:* 3 percent hydrogen peroxide is super for removing blood stains, especially if they are fairly fresh. For stubborn stains, combine ½ cup of hydrogen peroxide with 1 teaspoon of ammonia. Safe for whites and colorfast clothes. Always test on colored clothes before proceeding.

- *Lemon juice:* This is nature's bleach and disinfectant. If you have spots on white clothes, apply lemon juice and lay them out in the sun. Apply a little more lemon juice prior to laundering and launder as usual. Very effective on formula stains.

- *Meat tenderizer:* To remove protein-based stains such as milk, blood, egg, etc., apply cold water to the spot and sprinkle on the unseasoned meat tenderizer. Let it soak about an hour and launder as usual.

- *Shampoo:* Any brand. Work it into ring-around-the-collar and cosmetic stains for quick removal.

- *Shaving cream:* One of the best spotters available, because it is really whipped soap! If you have a spill on clothes (or even carpet), moisten the spot with cool water and work in a little shaving cream, then flush with cool water. Even if it doesn't remove the total spot, it won't set it, so you can still remove it with another method.

45

DO LAUNDRY

HELOISE

*

Heloise is a columnist for Good Housekeeping *and*
international newspaper syndication. She is the
author of numerous books, including
Heloise Conquers Stinks and Stains.

WASHING machine cycles or settings vary from machine to machine. Here are the standard ones:

- *Hand-wash or delicate:* A gentle action for fine lingerie or material. Less agitation than other settings.
- *Permanent press:* For materials that wrinkle easily. This setting will lessen the need for ironing.
- *Normal:* For lightly soiled garments and safe for most materials.
- *Heavy-duty:* For sturdy fabrics like work clothes that are deeply soiled or dirty.

1. PREPARE LAUNDRY

- Separate light-colored clothing from darker garments and do not wash together in the same load; the dyes of the darks can bleed onto the paler fabrics.
- Never wash or dry lint-making garments, such as bath towels, with lint-collecting ones, like permanent-press or synthetic clothes.
- Examine clothing for new and old stains. Read the care labels on the garments on how to treat before tossing into the machine. If you don't, that embarrassing dressing stain may remain on the front of your shirt.
- Zip zippers, clear out pockets, and shut snaps to prevent garment damage.

2. THE WASHING MACHINE

- Set the machine to the right level, time, and water temperature (hotter is not always best) for the clothing.
- Turn on the machine, and as the water rises in the tub, add the designated amount of detergent. Let the detergent mix (or dissolve) in the water.
- Then place the garments into the machine one piece at a time by laying them in a circle around the agitator. Do not overload because the clothes need space for proper cleaning and rinsing.

3. DETERGENTS AND BLEACHES

There are a wide variety of products geared to cleaning your clothing. Read the labels carefully. Here are some of the basics:

DETERGENTS

- *Liquids* work best in removing oily soils and for pretreating.
- *Powders* are effective in lifting out ground-in dirt and clay.
- *General-purpose* is appropriate for all washable fabrics.
- *Light-duty* can be used for hand or machine washing of lightly soiled garments and delicate fabrics.
- *High-efficiency (HE)* detergent is formulated for HE front-loading washers.

BLEACHES

- *Chlorine* should be used primarily on white clothing if the label allows. Do not put on acetates, silk, spandex, wool, or some flame-retardant fabrics.
- *Oxygen bleach* is *not* chlorine bleach—it is safe to use on most colored washable fabrics. However, the liquid form may work as a slower, milder bleaching agent and can be a laundry booster when used with detergent. The dry, powdered form works in much the same way. One important note: the hotter the water, the quicker oxygen bleach works. Most important, if the care label reads "Do Not Bleach," even oxygen bleach may not be recommended.

If your clothes come out with detergent still on them, rewash the load at the highest water level, without detergent.

4. THE DRYER

- Fabrics that shouldn't go in the dryer include: silk, spandex, wool, fine garments, and waterproof items.
- Always clean the lint filter before putting clothes inside (a clogged filter can be a fire hazard). Set the dryer on the appropriate setting for the load.
- Shake out damp items before putting into the dryer. Don't overstuff because the laundry will take longer to dry and will wrinkle more. Never add wet items to a half-dried load.
- Remove immediately to prevent wrinkles. You can hang up many garments and avoid ironing.

5. PUTTING LAUNDRY AWAY

- Fold socks when you take them out of the dryer to save time. Fold towels and roll them to save space in a small closet.
- After you've finished washing, drying, and folding clothes, put them under a current stack (underwear, T-shirts, towels, sheets, etc.), so they will be rotated; alternating use will make these items last a lot longer.
- When you store linen or clothing, add several used fabric-softener sheets between the stacks to help stop musty smells, but never let them touch silk. A wrapped bar of soap will do the job too.

46

IRON A SHIRT

Mary Ellen Pinkham

*

Mary Ellen Pinkham is the host of
TIPical Mary Ellen *on HGTV and a columnist for*
iVillage. *The newest of her many books is*
Don't You Hate It When . . .

THERE ARE people who iron and people who don't. But by midmorning, they both look pretty much the same. Few domestic tasks have as short-lived a payoff as ironing.

So what persuades people to take on what Erma Bombeck described as her second most favorite household chore, "the first being hitting my head on the top bunk until I faint"? It must be the feeling of slipping into a freshly ironed shirt: it's always shapely and perfect, even if the shirt's owner is not.

The best ironing tip is to put the board in a convenient location and give it a new, padded cover. Padding makes ironing easier.

To iron all-cotton, set the temperature high; lower for part (or all) synthetics. There's a guide on the iron. I haven't yet found a modern iron that gets hot enough to scorch a shirt (some are barely hot enough to iron one), but some synthetics melt at high temperatures, so take a test glide in a hidden area.

The key to a good ironing job is that the shirt should be slightly damp. Remove it from the dryer before it's bone dry. And if you can't get to it right away, stick it in a plastic bag in the freezer. It won't mildew, but it will stay damp.

If a shirt needs misting, don't rely on the spray reservoir built into the iron. Most of these need frequent refills, may clog up, and don't cast the spray very effectively. I recommend using a separate spray bottle, preferably one filled with a fragrant, flake-free product.

Finally, you need an ironing plan. The basic idea is to start with the smaller sections of the shirt first, because whatever section you are not working on tends to wrinkle up while you iron another part. Below is the suggested order:

1. *Collar:* Lay it flat, wrong side up, pressing from the points toward the center. Then press it on the right side.
2. *Yoke:* The yoke is the panel that covers the shoulders. Lay it over the widest part of the ironing board to do the job.
3. *Cuffs:* Iron the insides, then the outsides.
4. *Sleeves:* Smooth the sleeve flat with your palm and iron it, then flip it over and do the other side. Then do the other sleeve.

5. *Back:* Lay it on the wide part of the ironing board, too.

6. *Front panels:* Start with the pocket, then do the panels. The little grooves on your iron help you press around buttons.

7. *Finish:* Retouch the collar if it needs it, then hang the shirt until it's cool and dry before you put it in the closet. And don't jam it into your closet or you'll have to start all over again—which, of course, will happen soon enough.

*

47

SEW A BUTTON

SUSAN KHALJE

*

Susan Khalje is the host of DIY Do-It-Yourself Network's Sew Much More *series. She is the author of two books, including* Bridal Couture: Fine Sewing Techniques for Wedding Gowns and Evening Wear. *She is the founder and director of the Couture Sewing School.*

I F you're replacing a button that's come off, it's easy to locate where to re-sew it: look for any remaining threads, or for holes left by the old thread. If the button has pulled off and weakened the fabric, or taken a little fabric with it, you'll have to re-position it slightly.

If you're sewing a button onto lightweight fabric (a cotton shirt, for example), ordinary sewing thread will do; otherwise, use stronger thread (carpet thread, waxed linen thread, or even dental floss). Use double thread, about 15 inches long; make it longer if you're sewing more than one button.

Attaching a sew-through button (the kind on most shirts) is pretty logical. But if the button is sewn too closely to the fabric, there's no room for the fabric to fit underneath, making it hard to button and forcing the fabric to bunch up. To avoid this, you'll want to create a thread shank between the button and the fabric, which will allow room for the fabric that's going to surround the button once it's in use.

Start by securing the thread to the fabric. You could knot it, but to avoid a big knot on the underside of the fabric, start by making a few small stitches on the top of the fabric, just where you're going to put the button, to anchor the thread (A). Hold the thread ends in place with the thumbnail of

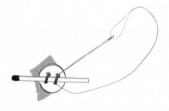

PICTURE A

your free hand. Once they're anchored, you can trim off the loose ends.

After securing the thread, place the button on top of the fabric, and bring the needle up through one of its holes. Before you put the needle back down through another hole, put a matchstick, a toothpick, or even a straight pin on top of the button and sew over it (B). This will create slack in the

PICTURE B

thread, which you'll use shortly to create the shank. Go back and forth 6 or 8 times, then remove the matchstick, tug the button away from the fabric, and you'll see that the extra thread has created a shank between the button and the fabric.

Strengthen the shank by wrapping your thread around it a few times (C), then secure the thread by running your needle in and out of the base of the shank a few times. Finally, take the needle to

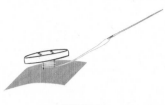

PICTURE C

the back of the fabric—right under the button—and make a few small final stitches. Pull the thread snug, and trim the threads.

If one of your shirt buttons is missing, you can poach one from the bottom front of the shirt. Dress shirts are almost always tucked in, so you probably won't miss the lowest button. Often, extra buttons are sewn inside garments, and there may be inner buttons that can be borrowed for the more visible parts of the garment.

Sometimes the only thing to do is replace all the buttons on your garment. Just be sure the new buttons are the right size for the buttonholes. Now that you know how to sew them in place securely, you'll never lose them again!

*

48

PICK PRODUCE

PETE NAPOLITANO

*

Pete Napolitano, aka "Produce Pete," is the produce
expert on NBC TV stations in New York and Philadelphia.
He is the author of Produce Pete's Farmacopeia.

BEING familiar with what's in season is your first step in picking and buying good produce. Buying too early or too late in the season always leaves you disappointed. Ask your produce person in the stores or do a little homework (see below) and you'll have much better luck selecting good produce. Just because something looks perfect, it won't necessarily taste good. A winter tomato can be perfectly round and uniformly colored, but it's not going to taste like anything. Your other senses—especially your nose—are going to tell you as much about fruits and vegetables as your eyes will.

The key is knowing what's in season in your area. I love waiting with my tongue hanging out for the in-season fruits and vegetables to arrive. Here are some of the hardest fruits and vegetables to pick.

CANTALOUPES

Look at the stem end and make sure none of the stem is still attached. Next, look for a cantaloupe with a golden color and a sweet fragrance. The time for cantaloupes is June through September, with July and August being the best. Refrigerate a cantaloupe only after you cut it and wrap it, because it will pick up every taste that you have in the refrigerator. A cantaloupe will keep from 3 to 5 days on the kitchen counter, and it tastes better at room temperature.

HONEYDEWS

Honeydews ripen from the center out and have a very thin rind. A good, sweet honeydew will be a little grainy on the skin and have a stickiness. Of all the melons, the honeydew is the most aromatic, so just give it a smell. If it smells sweet, it will taste sweet. Leave it on the counter for at least 1 day to get the cold out. The best time for honeydews is August through October. A good honeydew before August 1 is as rare as a blue moon. Refrigerate a honeydew only after you cut it or when you can feel the stickiness come through the melon. A honeydew will keep from 3 to 5 days out of the refrigerator, depending on the ripeness.

WATERMELONS

Check the stem of the watermelon. If it's green, the watermelon isn't ripe. If the stem is completely missing, it's probably overripe. A shrunken or discolored stem still attached to the watermelon usually means it's ripe. Turn the watermelon over and look for a yellowish belly and, most important, give it a pluck with your finger or a tap with your hand to make sure it has a solid sound. That's what you're look-ing for. Three-quarters of the crop is produced between June and August, with July being the best month. Store a watermelon in a cool place and refrigerate once it is cut. Whole watermelons last for weeks, but once cut, they will only last 1 or 2 days in the fridge.

STONE FRUIT: PEACHES, PLUMS, NECTARINES, APRICOTS

The problem with most stone fruit is over-refrigeration. Keep these fruits out of the "Killing Zone" of temperatures (36 to 50 degrees Fahrenheit) until they are soft. Most stores where you buy your fruit—and the trucks that transport the fruit—are refrigerating the fruit to death, which makes it dry and mealy. Choose fruit that is unbruised, colorful, and firm but that will give to a gentle squeeze. When you bring your fruit home, place it in a paper bag and close the bag. Leave for only 1 day, and it should ripen nicely. Stone fruit is available from May through September. In May and June, the fruit is still too green, and in September, too dried out. So enjoy July and August. Refrigerate only when ripe and only for a short time; refrigeration dries out the fruit. Ripe stone fruit is highly perishable and will keep for only 1 or 2 days.

TOMATOES

A good-tasting tomato needs to have some maturity when it's harvested, so look for one with a break of color, meaning it should show a little pink to red. Choose tomatoes that are not hard. Ripen on the counter—never in the sun—and *never refrigerate*. Refrigeration kills the flavor and texture of a good tomato. Tomatoes are available year-round but tastiest in the summer months.

EGGPLANT

Look for eggplants that are firm and have a shiny skin with a fresh, green spiky cap. Take the eggplant in your hand and press it with your thumb. If it leaves a thumb impression, pass it by; it is usually old. Peeling the eggplant helps reduce the bitterness. Eggplants are perishable. Don't refrigerate, but do keep them in a cool place where they will turn brown. Eggplants are available year-round, but the ones in the summer are fresher.

*

49

MARK BITTMAN

BUY FISH

*

Mark Bittman is a food columnist for the
New York Times *and the author of numerous books,*
including How to Cook Everything *and* Fish:
The Complete Guide to Buying and Cooking.

WITHOUT becoming obsessive, you are not going to learn the names or nature of every type of fish. What you can do, however, is follow a few guidelines that will guarantee that the fish you buy is of high quality.

First of all, know this: if the fillets or steaks of two fish look about the same, they will cook and taste about the same. Red snapper and black sea bass, steelhead trout and salmon, petrale sole and fluke—these have different names, but they'll behave the same in the kitchen and at the table. Don't go to the store fixated on a particular fish, but do go wanting a *type* of fish, like thick white fillets, or something in the salmon family. You'll be less frustrated and be able to select whatever's looking best.

SHOPPING

First, if a store smells fishy, or isn't clean, or skimps on ice, go to a different store. Next, consider buying the fish that looks best.

Fillets and steaks should be firm, shiny, glistening, even, and unmarred. Ask the seller to poke it: the flesh should spring back quickly—dents are not good. Smell it too: the smell should be of fresh seawater; if it smells bad, it can't taste good. Whole fish is easier: gills should be bright red, and the skin should gleam; the best whole fish look almost alive.

Shellfish (shrimp, lobsters, crabs, and other crustaceans) and mollusks (clams, mussels, oysters, and scallops) are another story. If they are in their shells, they should be either alive or cooked. Lobsters and crabs should be active. There's a difference between "alive" and "fresh," and you want both; a lobster that has been sitting in a tank without food for three weeks may be alive, but it is certainly not fresh.

Clams, oysters, and mussels should have undamaged shells that are nearly impossible to pry open with your fingers. They should never be stored in a closed plastic bag—they will suffocate and spoil quickly. At home, store them, dry and uncovered, in a pot or bowl. Shucked mollusks—scallops are almost always sold this way—should simply smell and look good.

Almost all shrimp are frozen before sale. And you might as well buy them frozen so that you have the convenience of defrosting them when you need them, rather than when the supermarket wants to sell them.

Frozen fish can also be a good choice. Would you rather have a fish that was caught, then stored in a hold for a few days, transferred to a truck, a warehouse, another truck, and then to the supermarket, which might be 10 days or more after capture? Or one that was caught and frozen the same day? If you're sure about the quality of the "fresh" fish you're buying, great; but if you're not, frozen fish is likely the better option.

STORING

Finally, storing fish is an important adjunct to buying it. Never keep fish in a hot car, even for an hour (an insulated bag in the trunk, even without ice, can help), and keep it chilled at home. If you're not going to cook it the same day, it pays to bury the fish, still wrapped, in ice; vegetable bins are good for this. You paid for it; you might as well protect your investment.

*

50

PAINT A ROOM

BOB VILA

*

Bob Vila is the host of Bob Vila's Home Again *and*
former host of PBS's This Old House. *He is the*
author of ten books, including Bob Vila's
Complete Guide to Remodeling Your Home.

O V E R the past twenty-five years I have had the privilege to restore, remodel, and build many great American homes. One of the most common questions that I have been asked is "How do you paint a room?" While the temptation is to grab a brush and get started, doing a little homework before you begin will ensure a project to be proud of when you are finished.

1. CHOOSE YOUR PAINT TYPE

Gloss paints, often called high-gloss finishes, have a highly reflective appearance. They produce the toughest, most durable, and most stain-resistant finishes. Because they are easier to clean than less reflective or low-luster paints, they are ideal for areas exposed to heavy traffic or use, especially those prone to fingerprints or grime. However, because of their highly reflective appearance, gloss paints tend to highlight surface imperfections. So if your walls or woodwork are marred or irregular, you might want to select paint with a lower sheen level. *Semi-gloss paints* are less reflective than gloss paints and have a slightly glossy appearance. They offer good stain resistance and are easy to clean.

Eggshell, satin, or *low-luster paints* have a sheen level that is even lower than semi-gloss, yet more lustrous than flat paints. Paints in this category impart greater warmth and depth to surfaces than flat paints. *Flat paints* are nonreflective, so they tend to conceal surface imperfections better than paints with higher sheen levels. This finish is especially good for walls that are dented or rough. Likewise, flat paints are a good choice for ceilings.

Matching the right paint to the surface will make a big difference in the longevity of your finished project.

2. MEASURE AND CALCULATE COVERAGE

Begin by measuring the dimensions of the surface area to be painted, and then multiply the height by the width. Perform the same calculation for areas that will not be painted, like doors and windows. Then subtract nonpaint areas like windows and open doorways (but don't forget that you probably will paint the door itself) from the overall surface area to determine the square footage you need to paint. The number of square feet a can of paint will cover in one coat is listed on the can's label. Divide the total surface area by this number to determine the number of gallons you will need for each coat. Quality paints cover about 400 square feet per gallon. Porosity (the size and number of tiny holes in the surface) also affects how much paint is needed, so optimal coverage and the number of gallons required will vary depending on the surface.

3. PREPARE PROPERLY

Resist that temptation to start painting right away. Before you start, remember that time spent on preparation will pay off in the final results. Wash walls with detergent to remove dirt, grease, oil, and fingerprints; a floor sponge mop makes a handy wall washer. Rinse thoroughly and wait until everything is completely dry before painting. If possible, remove furniture from the room. If not, place it in the center of the room and cover it with drop cloths. Remove electrical plug and switch covers. Mask off trim and moldings with painter's masking tape.

4. PAINT!

Now for the easy part—applying the paint. I recommend starting with the highest point, the ceiling. Brush out the wall/ceiling edges, then roll on ceiling paint. Keep your finish strokes in the same direction for uniformity.

Before you start with a paint roller, "cut in" a few inches with a brush around windows, doors, molding, and woodwork, and in the corners. A 2-inch brush works well for working around edges and corners, while 3- and 4-inch brushes work well for general interior painting.

Once all the detail work is done, it is time to paint the walls. A high-quality smooth ¼-inch- or semi-smooth ⅜-inch-nap roller cover works best. Start in an upper corner and work down, being careful not to overspread the paint. Each roller load should cover about 2 feet by 2 feet. Repeat with the next section until you've covered the room.

The last step is to paint the window frames, muntins (the small bars separating the glass in a window), sashes, and other trim and molding. Use a sash and trim brush for detail work. A sash and trim brush is typically 1 to 2½ inches wide with an angle edge that makes it easier to work in tight corners.

5. ONE FINAL TIP

It is better to buy more paint than you think you will need than to run out before the job is done. Purchasing all your paint at once will help ensure can-to-can color consistency and save time on trips to the store. If you have leftover paint, you can always use it for touch-ups. Unused and unopened paint may be returned for credit, unless it is a custom color.

*

51

HANG A PICTURE

BARBARA KAVOVIT

✳

*Barbara Kavovit is CEO of Barbara K Enterprises,
Inc., a company that specializes in creating solution-
oriented products that "give women the tools to
succeed." She recently launched several lines of products
designed specifically for women. She is currently writing
a book and developing a television program.*

HANGING a piece of artwork or picture is an easy way to dramatically change the appearance of a room, and it's a home-enhancement project you can do in under a half hour.

The most time-consuming part is deciding where to hang the art. First, consider the scale of the room. Group small pieces together, or use a large piece as a focal point. Centering art over a sofa or other furniture with the frame 5 to 8 inches above the furniture makes a dramatic statement. And don't forget about lighting. Overhead incandescent lights at subdued settings emphasize artwork and minimize glare. Valuable art should not be hung in direct sunlight (or above fireplaces, in kitchens, or in bathrooms, for that matter).

If you need more help imagining how the picture will look in place, outline the piece on paper and use low-tack tape to stick it to the wall for an instant visual. Generally, the center of the piece should be at eye level, roughly 5 feet from the ground.

Once you've decided on perfect placement and lighting, get your tools. You'll need a hammer, adhesive tape, a tape measure, a pencil, a level, and a picture hook. (Be sure to use a hook that can hold the weight of the picture.) Your hardware store should have a variety of hooks—the kind with the nail set at a 45-degree angle is best for most walls. If the picture does not already have wire on the back, you'll also need picture wire that can bear 30 pounds of pressure and a couple of small eyelet screws to secure the wire to the frame. Leave enough "give" in the wire to allow gravity to do its job. The eye hooks should be placed into the center of each side (left, right) of the frame. For large pictures, they should be placed 8 inches from the top, for medium, 6 inches from the top, and for small, 2 to 4 inches from the top.

Use your pencil to make a mark on the wall where you will be placing the nail—about 5 feet from the ground. Now you're ready to pick up the hammer. But before you land that first blow, do yourself a favor and put a small piece of adhesive tape over that pencil mark. This will eliminate any cracking, especially in a plaster surface. Once you've got the spot taped, then use your hammer to gently tap the picture hook into place. Check that the hook is secure and hang your picture.

Now step back. Make sure your picture is straight by taking the level and resting it on top of the frame. Even if it looks straight to the naked eye, your perception may be thrown off by a slightly settled foundation or the optical illusion of a crooked piece of molding. Trust that level (you simply have to shift the picture around until the bubble is in the middle) and, voilà—you've just become your own handyman or do-it-yourself diva!

*

52

WRITE A PERSONAL NOTE

LANSING E. CRANE

*

Lansing E. Crane is the chairman and
CEO of Crane & Co., Inc.

SENDING a personal note is the opportunity to pay tribute for a thoughtful gift or an act of kindness, or to share in a time of happiness or sorrow. A personal note can and should be an important emotional connection between the writer and the recipient.

Before you begin writing, there are a few basics to consider:

- *Timing:* Once the occasion arises, write your note as soon as possible. You don't want to begin your note with an apology, and you want the emotion you experienced to be as fresh as possible.
- *Paper:* Write your note on the best paper available. The sentiment of a personal note is actually a gift from the writer. Wrap that gift in fine paper—it will add to your recipient's emotional experience.

- *Content:* Focus on why you're writing. Look for the emotional connection that is leading you to put pen to paper.
- *Length:* Personal notes don't have to be long. Keep them simple, but sincere.

THE BEGINNING

Starting your note should be easy. If it's a thank-you note, start with these two words: "Thank you," and just state why you're saying it: "for the beautiful pair of candlesticks"; "for the wonderful weekend at the beach house"; "for your kind note after Dad passed away." If there's another reason why you are writing, such as to offer congratulations or condolences, begin with that.

THE MIDDLE

Your second sentence should establish the personal, emotional connection to the recipient, as in these examples:

- "Peter and I just finished a quiet dinner together, illuminated by your thoughtful gift."
- "Although we won't be able to have a clambake on the shore, we look forward to your visit to the city so we can return your wonderful hospitality."
- "I know you never had the chance to meet Dad; you two would have enjoyed each other's company."

THE CLOSING

Before you start your note, you should decide how to finish it so you know where you are going before you start putting pen to paper:

- "We promise to use them for only the most special occasions."
- "I hope the rest of your summer is filled with sunshine and warm breezes."
- "It's a great comfort in this difficult time to have such a good friend."

And that's it. You and the recipient of your note will be emotionally closer, all because of a little thoughtfulness expressed on fine paper.

*

53

MAKE TEA

MO SIEGEL

*

Mo Siegel is the founder and former chairman and
CEO of Celestial Seasonings. He is the
co-author of Herbs for Health and Happiness:
All You Need to Know.

SINCE ITS discovery over 5,000 years ago, tea has become an integral part of our lives. For some, brewing and drinking tea is an art form. According to a Japanese proverb, "If man has no tea in him, he is incapable of understanding truth and beauty."

Making tea is as simple as boiling water, but to make your cup of tea the best cup requires a few special steps.

STEPS FOR BREWING THE BEST CUP OF HOT TEA

1. *Use fresh water:* Good water makes good tea, so start with fresh, cold water.
2. *Heat the water:* For black and herb teas, use boiling water. For green tea, heat the water just to the boiling point.
3. *Pour the water over the tea bag:* Immediately pour the boiling water into your teapot or teacup, over the tea bag.

4. *Cover your cup:* Whenever possible, keep the teacup or teapot covered to retain the heat.

5. *Time the brew:* For best flavor, brewing time depends on the tea type: 3 to 5 minutes for green teas and black teas, 4 to 6 minutes for herb teas, and 6 minutes for wellness teas.

6. *Squeeze the bag:* Give the tea bag a gentle squeeze to release the last bit of flavor and color, then remove the bag from the cup or pot.

7. *Prepare to enjoy:* If desired, the tea flavor can be complemented with a favorite sweetener (I like honey) and/or lemon. For black tea, milk may be used (cream is too heavy for most tea varieties). Traditionally, green tea is served without milk. Also, most herb teas taste best without milk, especially fruit and mint varieties. Check the tea package for specific preparation recommendations.

STEPS FOR BREWING THE BEST CUP OF ICED TEA

To make one quart:

1. Pour 2 cups of boiling water over 4 tea bags (for green teas, use water heated just to boiling).
2. Steep 4 to 6 minutes.
3. Remove the tea bags (or not).
4. If desired, stir in a sweetener while the tea is hot.
5. Add 2 cups of cold water and chill.
6. Serve over ice.
7. Garnish with fresh fruit or mint.

For a stronger brew, use more tea bags. Iced tea tastes best if used within 72 hours of brewing.

54

CORY BOOKER

READ ALOUD

* * *

*Cory Booker is a Newark-based politician and social
activist who makes more than four hundred public
appearances annually. A zealous advocate for young
people across the country, he spends much of his time
working with at-risk children in schools and
community outreach programs, where he has ample
opportunity to practice the art of reading aloud.*

WHILE I give many readings a week, at times I still get nervous. I remain a bit connected to that fourth-grader who was asked to read aloud in Mrs. Magner's social studies class. Now older and over the devastation of those classroom embarrassments, I have found a few key things that have greatly helped me when asked to read out loud (if only I could go back and read about Nanook of the North again).

1. BREATHE, BREATHE, BREATHE!

I cannot emphasize this enough. Eastern faiths see mindful breathing as the gateway to profound peace and strength, and even Western doctors document the benefits for relaxation and emotional confidence. Breathing is the source of life, and for those of us who must read out loud, though it may not help us reach Nirvana, it is essential for outstanding oration.

2. BE COMFORTABLE AND CALM

Before reading, make sure you are comfortable and calm. Pause, take slow deep breaths, relax, and focus on your material. Becoming anxious or nervous will only adversely affect the way you speak. If the eyes are the window to your soul, then your voice—its tenor, speed, strength, and volume—is a projection of your mood and attitude. You want your listeners to hear the substance of what you are reading, empowered by your spirit and confidence; you don't want them distracted by rushed nervousness or insecurity and discomfort.

3. KNOW AND PRACTICE YOUR MATERIAL

Though not always possible, it is absolutely best to know your material and to have practiced reading it out loud. Like jogging through the woods, you proceed more confidently when you know the path. If you don't know the material, take a few moments to read or scan the page before you begin. In even a few moments, your eyes will pick up things in the text, and you will benefit from the familiarity with greater confidence and hints on how to use your voice most effectively.

4. READ WITH AUTHORITY

Once you have begun reading, do so with authority. As my football coach once told me, "Nothing sucks more than a soggy tissue." I believe he was trying to tell me to be confident and strong. Control your breathing, read slowly, and project your voice from deep in your gut (not your throat).

Whether reading a bedtime story or a passage or presenting a sales pitch, let your listeners hear your passion. Take your time to enunciate and project each word. Enjoy what you are doing—luxuriate in it.

Don't read in a monotone. Do change your vocal inflections and subtly vary speed to add color and emphasis. Speak slowly, be purposeful, and always have the tone in your voice reflect what you are reading.

5. MAKE EYE CONTACT

Make eye contact with your audience from time to time, but only if you feel comfortable. It is better to make an excellent presentation than to allow yourself to be thrown off.

Finally, if you mess up, so what! Don't let it shake you. Smile, take a breath, correct the mistake, and keep going. Go Nanook!

WEEKEND
LIFE

55

RELAX

DEAN ORNISH

*

Dr. Dean Ornish is the author of numerous best-selling books, including Dr. Dean Ornish's Program for Reversing Heart Disease. *He is the founder and president of the nonprofit Preventive Medicine Research Institute and a clinical professor of medicine at the University of California, San Francisco. He was the first to prove that heart disease can be reversed by comprehensive lifestyle changes, including diet and meditation.*

THOUGH relaxation is often considered a luxury, there is increasing scientific evidence that it is at least as important as exercise in maintaining good health. Here are the steps.

BREATHE

Deep breathing works to help prevent harmful reactions to stress and to relieve them. Even when you can't control the situation, you can always control your breathing and thus change your reaction to unpleasant circumstances. Deep breathing can be done anywhere, at any time, and practice makes it even more effective. Since exhaling is the most relaxing phase of breathing—*aahhh*—take longer to exhale than to inhale. Many teachers advise that a 2:1 ratio is ideal—take twice as long to exhale as to inhale when you're feeling stressed.

MEDITATE

Meditation is the practice and process of paying attention and focusing your awareness. Even a few minutes a day can bring great benefits. When you meditate, a number of desirable things begin to happen— slowly, at first, and deepening over time:

- First, when you focus your awareness, you gain more power. When you focus your mind, you concentrate better. When you concentrate better, you perform better and can accomplish more—in the classroom, the boardroom, or the athletic arena. Whatever you do, you do it more effectively when you meditate.
- Second, a number of desirable changes occur in your body as you experience a profound state of relaxation, deeper even than sleep. These include decreased blood pressure, a slower heart rate, dilating of your arteries, and clearer thinking.

- Third, you enjoy your senses more fully. Meditation can *enhance* your senses in ways that are profoundly sensual. Anything that you enjoy—food, sex, music, art, massage, and so on—is greatly enhanced by meditation. When you pay attention to what you eat, for example, you may need less food yet enjoy it more fully with greater pleasure.
- Fourth, your mind quiets down and you experience an inner sense of peace, joy, and well-being. When you experience this, you can be relaxed in the midst of the busiest activities. When you realize from your own experience that your peace comes from within, it can be profoundly empowering.

FOCUS

There are many different types of meditation found in all cultures throughout the world. While the forms vary, certain principles are universal.

In most forms of meditation, you repeat a sound, a phrase, or a verse from a prayer. It can be a sacred object such as rosary beads or a picture or icon. Or you can simply observe your breathing. In and out. Repeatedly.

Certain sounds are found to be very soothing. These sounds are often translated to mean "peace," like *Om* or *Shalom* or *Amen* or *Salaam*. If you are more comfortable with a secular meditation, you can repeat the word *One*. A mother or father humming to their baby has an intuitive understanding that a humming sound is very peaceful. These sounds usually begin with an *o* or an *ah* and end with an *m* or an *n*.

Meditation is both effortless and hard work—easy to learn but difficult to master. A wandering mind is part of the process. When you become aware that your mind is wandering, gently but firmly bring it back, without criticizing or berating yourself. With practice, you will find that your mind wanders less than before.

PRACTICE

Consistency is more important than duration. You might get so busy that you think you don't have time to meditate. But if you meditate for even just one minute, chances are you will continue doing it for longer. And even a minute has benefits. Have you ever listened to a song on the radio in the morning and found yourself humming it later in the day? Similarly, on a subconscious level, you continue meditating throughout the day.

MINDFULNESS

Observe whatever comes up in each moment, without judgment. Just watch your thoughts bubble up without getting caught up in the emotion or the content of them. Eventually, your life becomes a continual meditation, and you remain relaxed even in the busiest circumstances.

*

56

WASH A CAR

CHARLES OAKLEY

*

Charles Oakley is an NBA player with the Washington Wizards. He is also the owner of Oakley's Car Wash, a line of car washes on the East Coast.

KEEPING a car clean has a dramatic effect on its appearance. Over time, the effects of natural elements can adversely affect your vehicle's finish. One of the best ways to deter this deterioration is to keep the finish as clean as possible, with proper washing procedures.

There are a few basics to keep in mind to make the most out of washing your car.

THE WASH

- Before washing, find a good roomy space in which to work. Never wash the car in the sun or while the paint is hot, because this puts you at risk for soap drying on the car before you have a chance to rinse it off. This can be damaging to the paint.

- First, vacuum the interior thoroughly. Check for excess crumbs and dirt that are hidden between the console and in the cup holders. Wipe the dashboard and clean the cup holders and surfaces inside the car. Then air out the mats.
- Next, clean the tires and wheels. Pressure wash to clean inside the wheel wells. Brush and scrub any dirt off the wheels and rinse.
- Then, rinse the dirt and soil off the rest of the car so that it does not get rubbed in and cause scratches.
- Next, using a 100 percent cotton soft-cloth wash mitten or a high-quality sea sponge, wash the car from top to bottom, in straight lines and overlapping strokes.
- Don't ever use household liquid soaps, as these detergents can strip the protective wax coat. Instead, use a good liquid detergent that is specifically designed for cars.
- Make sure to rinse the sponge or cloth well before using, or dirt can get caught under it and scratch the paint. Continue to wash the entire vehicle with special attention to dead, dried bugs, road tar, tree sap, and bird droppings.
- Run your wash mitten along the inside bottom edge of the doors, lift gate, hood, and trunk. These areas trap dirt and moisture, which can cause premature rusting.
- Pressure wash to clean inside the wheel wells.
- Do use water in abundance. Take the nozzle off the hose when rinsing, and allow water to sheet off the car.

- Finally, when drying your car, open up all doors to enable semi-exposed areas to dry completely. Be sure to use an all-cotton towel to dry the car. Any other type of towel may have a sandpaper effect, creating scratches and swirls on the finish.
- Make sure to rinse your cloth thoroughly after each time you wash your car so as to prevent dirt and sand from remaining in it.

THE WAX

- To hand-wax a vehicle, use a foam applicator, which cannot harm the finish. Avoid products that promise to remove dirt, oxidized paint, or surface scratches, because they can have the opposite effect.
- Always wax in a cool place. Hot metal surfaces can cause the wax chemicals to damage the glossy finish. Also, if wax is applied in high humidity it may streak, leaving ugly lines.
- Make sure to wax small areas at a time, constantly rotating the cleaning towel to provide a fresh area for proper wax removal.

*

57

CHANGE A TIRE

Larry McReynolds

*

Larry McReynolds was a renowned pit-crew chief
with 23 victories, 21 pole positions, 122 Top 5
finishes, and 209 Top 10 finishes.
He is currently a broadcaster for Fox Sports.

K N O W I N G where everything is and how to operate it is the first step to success in changing your own tire. Be proactive and familiarize yourself on where the spare tire, lug wrench, and jack are located. Look at the instruction booklet on where to jack the car.

If you get a flat tire on the road, drive the shortest distance you can to prevent damage of the tire beyond repair, or damage to the wheel. Get as far off the roadway as possible—a parking lot is best. If you are forced to change the tire on the highway, get as far off to the side as you possibly can. But not into the woods: you want to avoid jacking the car up on a hill or on gravel, so try to find a flat area.

Put your car in park, put the emergency brake on, and be sure to put your emergency flashers on. Put out road flares, day or night, about 75 feet behind the car, far enough so that people can see them and slow down. If you are changing a tire on a curve, be sure to put the flares before the entrance to the curve.

Once you are in the safest location possible, determine which tire is flat. Get out the spare tire, jack, and lug wrench. One side of the lug wrench can be used to remove the hubcap: put it under the back edge of the hubcap and pry it off. Use the lug wrench to break the lug nuts loose by going counterclockwise; you can do this with the car still on the ground. But just loosen the nuts at this point; don't remove them.

Do not allow anyone to stay in the car while you jack it up. Place your jack in the proper position—if you jack in the wrong place, you could damage your car, or, even worse, it could tip over by coming off the jack. Once the car is jacked up, never put any part of your body underneath the car.

Now that the car is jacked up, go ahead and remove all the lug nuts the rest of the way, using the lug wrench. Remove the flat tire and set it aside. Take your spare tire and place it up on the hub. Line the spare up with the lug studs, push it on, and apply your lug nuts as tight as you can with your fingers. Then, take the lug wrench and tighten them as tightly as you can with the car still jacked up. Take the jack down.

Once the car is back on the ground and off the jack, double-tighten all the lug nuts in an alternating pattern rather than side by side. Make sure you hit every lug nut three or four times to make sure it is as tight as possible. Once you've done this, put the flat tire, jack, lug wrench, and hubcap in the trunk. Don't bother putting the hubcap back on. Smaller, space-saving spare tires are made only to get you to a service station where you can get your full-size tire repaired or replaced. Extinguish the flares prior to leaving. Cut your flashers off and be on your way.

PREVENTION

1. Every time you fill with fuel, check the air pressure in your tires. The proper pressure can be found on the sidewall of the tire.
2. Purchase a can of Fix-a-Flat. This cannot be used for a flat tire, but it can be used for a soft tire with a leak.
3. Check the tire pressure in your spare tire every time you get your oil changed.

*

58

CHANGE YOUR OIL

Ryan Newman

*

Ryan Newman is the NASCAR Nextel
Cup Series driver of the
No. 12 ALLTEL/Mobil 1 Dodge Intrepid.

Y OU DON'T have to be a NASCAR driver to know that you can keep your car running at peak performance by changing the engine oil as recommended by the owner's manual. Regular and routine car maintenance will extend the life of your car and, most important, save you money. Engine oil unchanged for too long can slow you down by leading to deposit and sludge buildup in your engine, reducing your car's performance and, ultimately, engine life.

BEFORE YOU GET STARTED

Choose a flat spot in your driveway, garage, or in my case, race shop, to park your car. Oil may leak, so be prepared to guard against spills with cardboard or a large tarp. You also will need to familiarize yourself with your vehicle, choose the right engine oil, and ensure that you have the proper tools and supplies at your disposal. Changing your oil will take approximately 30 minutes.

GET TO KNOW YOUR CAR

Check under your car to be sure you know where the oil pan, drain plug, and filter are located. In most cars, the drain plug will have a hexagonal head, and the oil filter will be on the side of the engine. Refer to your owner's manual if you get confused or don't know where something is located. Locate the engine-oil fill cap under the hood to install the new oil, and have the engine dipstick handy to measure the new oil level.

CHOOSE THE RIGHT ENGINE OIL

Your owner's manual offers specifics on the best type and amount of oil for your vehicle and the right-size oil filter. Oils come in different viscosity, weights, and formulations. To avoid confusion, always remember that synthetic oils provide the best overall performance for vehicles and driving conditions.

TOOLS AND SUPPLIES

1. *Owner's manual.*
2. *New oil:* Refer to your owner's manual for the recommended quantity and viscosity grade of new oil.
3. *New oil filters:* Your owner's manual will name the preferred size for your vehicle.
4. *Oil drain pan:* To catch your old, drained oil. Purchase one at your local auto parts store.
5. *Box or socket wrench:* Your local auto parts store can help you make the right choice.

6. *Oil filter wrench:* Buy a wrench that matches the size of the oil filter you purchase.
7. *Funnel:* This is handy for installing new oil.
8. *Dipstick:* Normally located under the hood of your car.

CHANGE THE OIL

Before you begin, make sure the car is turned off and the engine is warm. The car should be in park, or if you have a standard car, it should be in first gear, with the emergency brake set. Follow these steps:

1. Locate the oil pan and drain plug.
2. Place the drain pan under the drain plug. Remove the drain plug and allow the used oil to flow into the drain pan.
3. When draining is complete, replace the drain plug securely.
4. Remove the old filter and pour excess oil into the drain pan.
5. Dab some new engine oil on the gasket around the top of the new filter before you install it, to ensure easy removal next time. Screw in the new filter by rotating clockwise—do not screw in too tightly.
6. Once the filter is secure, pop your hood and remove the oil cap. Insert the funnel and add the new oil.
7. After oil is added, use your dipstick to measure proper levels as specified in your owner's manual. Overfilling can lead to leakage and cause car damage.
8. Check under your vehicle for leaks.
9. Start your engine, allow your car to idle briefly, and check again for leaks.

10. Remember to carefully dispose of your old oil. Save your oil bottles and place old oil in them for disposal. Check with your local government to help you dispose of the filter and used engine oil.

Changing your oil regularly is easy—it's so easy that you won't need my pit crew!

*

59

MOW A LAWN

DAVID MELLOR

✳

David Mellor is director of grounds at Fenway Park in Boston. He is the author of The Lawn Bible: How to Keep It Green, Groomed, and Growing Every Season of the Year *and* Picture Perfect: Mowing Techniques for Lawns, Landscapes, and Sports.

Y o u don't need a big fancy professional tractor mower to mow your lawn like a pro. The simplest push-style reel mower can give you as nice a cut as the most elaborate deck mower—or the most expensive lawn-care company you could hire. Just follow these simple guidelines.

Before you cut a blade of grass, there are three things you need to do:

1. *Check your equipment.* Make sure the blades on your mower are sharp. Dull blades tear the grass plants instead of cutting them, leaving them stressed, prone to weeds and disease, and

giving a ragged, bummed-out look to the lawn. You should sharpen your blades three times a season.

2. *Set your blades* so that they will cut no more than ⅓ off the top of the grass when you mow. This is known as the One-Third Rule. No matter how long the grass is—or how tempted you are to give it a nice, neat buzzcut—do not cut more than ⅓ of the grass plant at a mowing. If you do, you will weaken the root system of the grass and leave it vulnerable to weeds, disease, and heat stress.

3. *Look at your lawn, not your calendar,* when deciding if it's time to mow. Simply put, cut the grass again when it has grown back to the height it was the last time you cut it. Even though it's easier to make a date with yourself for every Saturday at 2:00 P.M. to mow the lawn, you really should be letting the lawn tell you when to mow—that is, when it's grown to ⅓ taller than its ideal height. And that growth depends on your lawn's general health, the amount of sun and rain you've had, and your fertilizing habits—not the calendar.

Here is the twelve-step plan for mowing your lawn:

1. For your safety and to protect your equipment, remove any debris (sticks, stones, etc.) before you begin mowing.
2. Check your blades to see that they're set at the correct height for the current length of your lawn. See the One-Third Rule above.
3. Begin by mowing one pass (your header strip) at the ends of your lawn and around trees, gardens, building, or other structures to give yourself some room for turning.

4. Cut straight rows between the headers.

5. Overlap each row by 2 or 3 inches to ensure total coverage.

6. Make gentle turns, lifting your mower deck as you turn so that the blades don't keep turning on the grass in the same spot as you maneuver the mower to make the turn.

7. Change your mowing direction every time you mow. Mow at a 45- or 90-degree angle to the last time you mowed. This prevents tire ruts from developing and helps the grass grow upright instead of sideways from a constant mow pattern.

8. Don't mow when the grass is wet. Clumps of wet grass will stick to your blades and slow you down. And you'll have to keep stopping to clean off the blades to get an even cut of the lawn.

9. Always push your mower. Don't pull it toward you if you'd like to keep your digits intact.

10. Don't mow in the heat of the day. Your grass will already be suffering from being cut—don't make it suffer from the heat and the cut.

11. Mow sloping parts of your lawn on the diagonal. Mowing horizontally or vertically on a slope is tricky and dangerous.

12. Maintain your equipment. Hose down the blades and the deck after every use, keep your blades sharp, check your gas and oil.

*

60

FLY A FLAG

WHITNEY SMITH

✳

Dr. Whitney Smith is the director of the Flag
Research Center as well as a lecturer and appraiser of
old flags. He is the author of Flag Lore of All
Nations *and twenty-two other flag books, editor of*
The Flag Bulletin *and vexillology.com, founder of the*
International Federation of Vexillological
Associations, designer of the national flag of Guyana,
and inventor of the term vexillology.

AN Y flag should be flown in a dignified fashion according to established protocol rules, unless disrespect is intended. For centuries, a flag flown upside down or at half-staff has been a form of nonviolent protest against disfavored programs, philosophies, and individuals. The U.S. Supreme Court has recognized the legitimacy of abusing or even destroying a flag in the exercise of First Amendment rights to free speech.

Other considerations arise in flag display, including choice of flag size, cleaning and/or repair of a flag, illuminating the flag (usually by spotlight) when in darkness, and the proper arrangement of multiple flags flown together. Americans tend to assume they have an unrestricted right to fly the Stars and Stripes. In fact, many condominium and apartment managers require residents to sign covenants forbidding use of any outdoor flags. Some communities limit business flag display, treating it as a covert form of advertising.

Flying the flag involves practical, legal, and social considerations. Flag dealers and flagpole riggers can assist with such technical aspects as raising and lowering flags or preventing their getting tangled when flying. For questions of proper etiquette and symbolism, a professional vexillologist, a scholar of flag history and protocol, is called for.

In the United States, commercially produced flags typically have grommets (brass rings) stamped into the heading, the strip of canvas running along the hoisting edge of the flag. The halyard (rope or cable) from which the flag flies has spring clips that can be attached to the grommets near the top and bottom of the heading. The halyard runs through a small pulley in the truck, a flat disk on the flagpole below the decorative finial. By pulling on one end of the closed loop formed by the halyard and flag, the flag can be raised or lowered.

Some flags (especially ones from Great Britain or the Commonwealth) have a cord sewn into the heading. These flags have a loop at the top and at the bottom, a small toggle. One end of the halyard has a toggle to fit within the loop on the flag, while the other end has a loop to accommodate the flag's toggle. This prevents a flag from being hoisted upside down, which can easily occur when the grommets-and-spring-clip system is used.

Small flags that are not intended for hoisting are usually permanently attached to a short staff for waving or for mounting in a wall bracket. Many office or parade flags have a sleeve along their hoist into which the staff slides. Screwheads on the staff fit over holes in the leather tabs sewn inside the sleeve to hold the flag in place. There are also special technical aspects of flag hoisting in maritime and military situations.

Normally, a flag is flown from the peak of a pole (mast, staff), but there are also special etiquette rules in certain situations. For example, on Memorial Day the U.S. flag goes briefly to the top of the pole when it is first raised and then flies at half-staff until noon. It is then flown full-staff until the end of the day.

Any flag threatened by stormy conditions (not just rain) should be removed. Traditionally, a flag no longer in fit condition is burned with or without ceremony. A damp flag should be dried out before being folded according to standard procedures. In long-term storage, the flag should not touch cardboard or wood (which are acidic); heat and direct light should also be avoided.

*

61

GARDEN

MAUREEN GILMER

*

Maureen Gilmer is the host of Weekend Gardening
on HGTV and the author of fifteen gardening books,
including Water Works: Creating a Splash in the
Garden. *She is also the author of*
Yard Smart, *a critically acclaimed syndicated column.*

SUCCESSFUL gardening always comes back to the basics:
soil, sun, oxygen, plants, and, most of all, water. Watering is the
key to everything in the garden world. Get this right and your garden goes crazy. Blow it and plants languish. Water allows the
uptake of fertilizer and nutrients through roots, thus connecting it
to soil. Water hydrates cells and tissues, which directly ties it to
the structure of the plant itself. Therefore, if you can water well,
everything else takes care of itself.

The following are a few rules that will keep your garden
thriving.

1. KNOW YOUR SOIL

Dig a 2-foot-deep hole in the yard and you'll find out what's really going on in your garden. The soil may be heavy and sticky, or soft and sandy. If you're lucky, it's a little of both. Now fill that hole with water. If it drains out in an hour, you have great drainage and water will easily penetrate. If it drains out in a day, it's about average. If it takes 2 days or more, you have heavy, slow-draining soil. This knowledge is essential to how you apply water to the ground.

2. DON'T WET THE DIRT

Ever water with your finger over the end of the hose to make it spray? If so, you're not watering; you're wetting the dirt. Virtually no moisture reaches plant roots beneath the surface. Watering by hand should be considered "flooding" because you must pour it on so the root zone is fully saturated.

3. DO WATER DEEPLY

In a healthy plant, the underground part is the root zone, roughly the same volume as that of the canopy, trunk, and branches. Plants that grew up on "wet the dirt" watering or sprinkler systems have roots only in the top few inches of soil. When the soil surface dries out, the plants suffer. Well-watered plants root much deeper and wider because their entire root zone has been regularly saturated. To promote a deep root system, concentrate water directly over the root zone. In heavy soils that absorb water very slowly, you must create an earth basin by using garden soil to create a berm 4 to 6 inches high around the base of the plant. It should be 6 to 12 inches out from the base of the trunk or stem. This holds the water until it can trickle down at its own rate.

4. DON'T SPRAY THE LEAVES

When watering in direct sun, avoid wetting the plant itself, and beware of splashing the lower leaves, which could reflect sun and lead to burning the leaf surface. If you want to wash dirt or dust off the foliage, do so only in the early morning or late evening when the sun is low in the sky.

5. DON'T DIG A HOLE

The Grand Canyon was created by fast-moving water. The full force of the garden hose can do the same in your soil. This exposes tender plant roots to the air, and they will dehydrate within an hour and die shortly after. Always use a diffuser nozzle set to "shower" or "rain" whenever you hand-water, providing a plentiful, even, and gentle flow, keeping soil where it belongs.

6. NEVER WATER ARBITRARILY

If you're in doubt about whether a plant needs water, dig a little hole to see what's going on down under. Wilted leaves occur because the plant can't get water up from the roots. The reason may be from roots lost to rotting in waterlogged soils or from roots lost to dehydration in super-dry soils. Clay soils that appear dry on top, even cracking, can be super-saturated just a few inches below. Don't rely on the surface to judge.

Each of these rules of watering is related to observation. They ask you to look at what's happening above and below ground before you pick up the hose. Learning how to water is indeed the best way to learn how to garden.

62

SWING A GOLF CLUB

JIM MCLEAN

✳

*Jim McLean is the owner of Jim McLean Golf Schools
and the director of Golf Instruction for KSL Properties,
including The Doral Resort and Spa. He is a former
PGA Teacher of the Year, author of numerous books,
including* The Eight-Step Swing, *and instruction editor
and senior advisor for The Golf Channel.*

MOST GOLFERS do not achieve a true swinging action
because they learn poorly from the beginning. To learn a golf
swing, you start small and build.

FIRST THINGS FIRST

Find a place to practice that has a putting green, a chipping area,
and a driving range. To accelerate your progress, we will start near
the hole and work back.

GOLF CLUBS

At first, you will not need a complete set. Make sure the grips are the correct size and the shafts are not too stiff, so that you can feel the club head.

EDUCATE YOUR HANDS

In golf, your only connection to the club is your hands. They control the clubface. A square clubface makes the ball go straight, closed makes the ball go left, and open makes the ball go right. Like any ball and stick sport, you need a good grip. In golf, your grip dramatically influences your ability to square the clubface at impact, so you must learn how to hold the club.

FIRST SHOTS

Once you have a good grip, your goal is to create a true swinging motion. Start with your putter and head to the putting green, or very closely mown grass. Strike putts at different lengths at no target. Strive for solid contact and a pure roll, meaning, do not attempt to get the ball in the air. Strike the equator of the ball and propel it forward, not up. When you take your stance, drop the putter on the ground and picture the target in your mind as you smoothly swing your dominant hand back in a bowling motion. Now pick up the putter and do the same thing.

MECHANICS

After you practice rolling the ball, you need to achieve a proper stroke and solid mechanics. A correct stroke should have the putter head swing back slightly up and inside the target line. The target line is from the ball to your intended target. After you contact the ball, the putter head swings back inside. You might think the putter should travel straight back and straight through, but it does not. Instead, the putter head travels on a small arc. This arc will hold true for all shots hit in golf.

THE ARC

The club head also swings upward after you hit the ball. At the completion of the backstroke, the club head swings down toward the ball. On a putt, swing through the center of the ball and then back up on the arc. It looks like this:

On your other golf shots hit with irons, the path looks like this:

For all of your golf shots, except for the driver and putter, remember that there is no attempt to lift the ball. You must learn to hit down as the drawing shows, by striking the ball with a downward blow. Hit the ball first, and then the ground. Burn this concept into your brain.

THE LEAD ARM AND WRIST

Train your lead arm and wrist as you begin chipping balls. The wrist must not break down through impact. Practice this striking move without a ball. It is similar to a backhand slap. To do this with a golf club the hands must lead the club head.

START SMALL

Build a small and correct swing by spending 90 percent of your available practice time near the putting green and chipping area. Watch the pros on television, or copy photos in magazines to achieve a solid golf stance and posture. A mirror will act as a tremendous coach. Use the mirror at home for short daily practice sessions.

FULL SWINGS

After gaining confidence on small shots and putts, you'll be ready to expand the swing. At this point, I recommend a series of lessons. Check out the instructors in your area and sign up for six lessons, one per week. Work on one thing each session and make sure to get in one playing lesson on the golf course. Many beginners do well by attending a golf school where they get full attention for two or three days.

KEEP IT SIMPLE

Golf is a complex sport, so I like to simplify it as much as possible. There is much to learn, and this takes time and a smart improvement plan. Do this and you will improve much more quickly and enjoy the game even more.

CONTINUING EDUCATION

Remember to learn the basics and then begin the journey to mastering them. Improvement comes much more quickly to students with a plan.

63

SWIM

SUMMER SANDERS

*

Summer Sanders emerged as the most decorated U. S. swimmer at the 1992 Olympic games in Barcelona, winning two gold medals, a silver medal, and a bronze medal. She is the cohost of NBA Inside Stuff *on ABC and the host of* The Sports List *on Fox Sports.*

THE EQUIPMENT

Get yourself a Speedo Lycra suit and make sure it is tight, as Lycra tends to stretch after several uses. A swim cap, any kind that is comfortable. Wetting the inside of the cap makes it easier to pull over your hair. To put on a swim cap, hold the edge of the cap (with the seam at the middle of the forehead) and pull hard over your head. Then simply stuff in all the excess hair. Goggles. You should try on several pairs and find one that fits your eyes and nose. Make sure they are snug to your eyes but not digging into the bridge of your nose.

Now that you look the part, on to the act of swimming. There are four strokes, and the one we will be focused on is freestyle, which is a side-to-side stroke. Imagine that you are a pig on a skewer. Your body has to rotate side to side while moving forward through the water. Use your arm pull and power from your kick to move your body forward.

THE ARM PULL

Your hand should enter the water first and slide forward in the direction you want your body to go. The rest of your arm should enter the water through that same line. As you begin to pull, use the distance from your fingertips to your elbow as a paddle and bring under your body. As you finish your pull, you should be rotating your hip and the other hand/arm should be entering the water. The power part of the pull is at the very end, but the strength comes from your initial grab and hold on the water. Remember that you are not simply pulling straight back. You want to make a movement that goes through the water. It's called "finding new water." There should be constant pressure on your paddles (hands) from the water.

KICKING

In this case, bigger is not better—small kicks are good. Efficient kicking should be your goal. Your feet should never spread more than a foot apart, and the power in the kick should come from the hips—not the knees. You can bend your knees to get a snap on your kick, but "bicycling" along will only slow you down. Remember that your leg muscles are the largest muscles in the body, so they use more oxygen. Use your legs wisely or they will make you very tired.

BREATHING

You should pick a pattern in which to breathe. I like every third stroke. This means you will be breathing to both sides and will help to keep your stroke balanced. To breathe, you need to blow most of your air out before you turn your head. This allows you to take in a big breath. Otherwise, you would have to blow out and breathe in in a short amount of time. When breathing, don't disconnect your head from your body. Remember the pig on a skewer analogy and don't pick your head up. Keep your head in the water so that as your body rotates, so does your head. Grab a breath, and your head then turns with the next rotation.

In all strokes, blow out your air gradually through your nose so as to keep the water out, but not all at once or you will sink. Air in the lungs works as a life preserver.

∗

64

HIT A TENNIS BALL

JENNIFER CAPRIATI

*

*Jennifer Capriati became a professional tennis player
at age thirteen. She holds an Olympic gold medal
and three grand slam titles.*

EQUIPMENT

Having the right equipment is essential to hitting a tennis ball.
Your racquet, grip, clothing, and shoes should be comfortable and
tight, but not too restricting. Choose a racquet that isn't too heavy,
is properly balanced, powerful, and at the same time one you can
control.

GRIP

The right grip will enable you to swing correctly and make proper
contact. The grip size should be just a little smaller than the width
of your hands in a closed fist. The best way for me to explain the
correct grip is to have you sit down in a chair. Lay a racquet on
your lap with the head of the racquet parallel to the ground. Place
your open hand perpendicular to the top of the handle. The handle

should be directly in the middle of the palm of your hand. Close your four fingers to grip the handle, thumb wrapped underneath. Now turn the racquet face up and hold it directly in front of you as if it were an extension of your arm. With your opposite hand, hold the throat of the racquet gently for support. Now, slightly adjust your hand to the right of the grip. Then cock the racquet up to a slight angle. Just about 20 to 30 degrees. If you're left-handed, everything would apply to the opposite hand.

STANCE

Stand with your feet shoulder-width apart, knees slightly bent, and your body leaning slightly forward so your weight is on the balls of your feet. Your arms should be comfortably in front of you with the racquet cocked up slightly and your left hand on the throat of the racquet for support. Do not grip the handle too tightly or your arm and hand will get tired. Stay a little bouncy on your toes so you can be ready to react to the ball. As you are looking ahead, face the net and your opponent. Watch where and when the ball leaves the opponent's racquet.

SWING

Let's assume the ball is coming to the forehand side. This is the stroke you hit with one arm, your stronger one. I will assume you are a righty. As the ball is coming toward you, take the racquet back and use the left arm to point to the ball to aid in maintaining eye contact with it. The head of the racquet should not go above your shoulders or below your waist. Take it back far enough so that it is just slightly out of your peripheral vision. When you make your move to hit the ball, turn your shoulders, waist, then feet sideways to adjust to the right distance to make contact with the ball. Now your legs should be slightly bent, shoulder-width apart so you can stay balanced. The right contact point is just in front of your right hip.

As the ball is coming toward you, rotate your hips slightly front-ward and move your arm with them at the same time. This is so you can get the momentum of your torso into the ball when you hit it, giving your shot more power. As you make contact, the racquet head should be perpendicular to the ground, hitting the ball as close to the center of the strings as possible. If the ball doesn't come toward you, you have to make adjustment steps with your feet to get in the perfect position to make contact. Finish the swing by bringing your right arm across your body and up over your left shoulder. Your head should stay still, and keep your eyes on the ball at all times!

After you finish the swing, turn your body to the net so that you are ready to hit the next shot. Remember to keep your eye on the ball and have happy feet. (This means always bouncing up and down so you can be ready and adjust to get set in the right position.)

The most important thing is to have fun! Tennis can be frustrating at first, but like everything, practice makes perfect.

65

GIVE A MASSAGE

DR. DOT

＊

Dr. Dot, aka Dot Stein,

is a masseuse to the stars.

M ASSAGE is the ultimate stress reliever, and it is easy to learn. Find a willing partner and try it out:

1. *Find some space:* No massage table? Find a few thick blankets and make room on the floor. Spread out the blankets. A cushioned massage table is best, but a floor is second best.
2. *Set the mood:* Make sure the room is warm and the lighting is soft. This helps the person receiving the massage relax. Always ask the person receiving the massage if he or she wants music.
3. *Dress or undress for comfort:* When giving a massage, it is best to wear loose-fitting clothing and sporty shoes, if any. Everyone involved with the massage should remove all jewelry. (Also, long fingernails are a no-no.) The recipient should choose whether or not to undress entirely.

4. *Tools:* Blankets, sheets, and towels for the recipient to lie on, and to cover the recipient; hair ties, to get all hair out of the way; massage oil, cream, or gel (lotion is a nightmare—it balls up constantly).

5. *Preparation:* Have the person lie face down (unless she is pregnant, in which case a chair massage is best). Always cover the whole body except the area you are focusing on.

6. *Lube time:* Start by rubbing oil into your own hands and warming it.

7. *Start your massage:* Begin with a person's back. It is the biggest area, and there is a lot of tension in the back and shoulders. Lean on your hands to make the strokes strong. Putting one hand on top of the other increases the pressure and feels great for the recipient. Always avoid the spinal cord. Drag your fingertips heavily up and down the back, just alongside the spine. Use your thumbs to firmly rub the muscle that runs from beneath the skull down to the shoulder. Go down the back without losing skin contact. Always have one hand on the body.

8. *Elbows:* If the person wants more pressure, use your forearm and elbow to rub the muscles, making sure to avoid bones.

9. *Legs:* After 20 minutes on the back, move to the legs. Kneel at the feet and use both hands to stroke up the leg, using body weight. Avoid too much pressure on the back of the knees. Knead the legs with both hands, covering all areas. Spoil your partner!

10. *Foot fancy:* Have the person lie on his or her back when massaging the feet. Place a pillow under the person's knees for

comfort. Use your thumbs to rub the arches firmly, and try to keep a strong touch to avoid tickling. Twist both hands firmly around the foot to work out tension.

11. *Handle with care:* Gently rub and stretch the neck from underneath, then use your fingertips to scrub the scalp as if you were a hairdresser washing someone's hair. Then put a tiny amount of oil onto your hands and gently massage the face. Be extremely gentle around the eyes and use firm, circular movements on the forehead to relieve headaches and tension. Be sure to massage all around the cheekbones and jaw. Gently pinch along the eyebrows, squeezing the stress out of them.

12. *Arms:* Gently tug on each arm before rubbing it down. Stroke firmly up each arm with your hands cupped, going deep on the muscle but light on the bones. Then move on to the hands. Gently tug on the fingers and do circular pressures around each joint with your thumb.

13. *Stomach:* When you massage the abdomen, be gentle but firm enough that it doesn't tickle. Place hands side by side on the lower abdomen, and slowly glide up toward the ribs. Then take both hands and glide over all the ribs and repeat. Be extra careful if the recipient is pregnant.

*

66

MAKE A MARTINI

DALE DEGROFF

*

Dale DeGroff, aka the King of Cocktails, is author of
The Craft of the Cocktail, *winner of the IACP Julia*
Child Award, and is considered America's foremost
mixologist. He honed his skills at New York's
Rainbow Room, among other venues.

WHEN Duke Ellington was asked whether he played jazz music, he mused, "There are only two kinds of music: good music and all the rest." Here is my music of the dry martini. You'll need 3 dashes of dry French vermouth and 2 ounces of London dry gin.

Pre-chill the glasses in the freezer. Fill the mixing glass with ice. A martini should always be mixed in a glass, not a metal container. Add the dashes of vermouth first, then the gin. Stir the ingredients with the ice—50 times if using large ice cubes, 30 times if using small cubes. We want water in the drink from the melting ice; it is a critical ingredient to mellow the alcohol's attack. Strain into a chilled, V-shaped 5½-ounce martini glass. Garnish with a pitted Spanish cocktail olive, and then twist a lemon peel over the top and drop it into the drink. And please, no more than 3 small olives in the glass. Additional olives should be placed on a small garnish dish to the side of the drink.

There are a few tricks to avoid disaster. Always store vermouth in the fridge. Even though it is fortified with brandy, it is still wine and will oxidize when left at room temperature. Large bottles left for weeks or months will go off even in the fridge, so buy smaller bottles of vermouth. If it sits too long between uses, cook with it! Buy good French dry vermouth. The bartender's maxim for over 100 years has been: use dry French vermouth for martinis and sweet Italian vermouth for Manhattans.

Don't use unfiltered tap water to make ice cubes. If your water is not filtered, use bottled water for ice cubes to avoid off flavors in your drinks.

Don't store gin in the freezer. Although it seems a natural thing to get the coldest possible martini, frozen gin will not melt the ice when stirring or shaking, and a little water in the drink is critical for a mellow, smooth martini.

That brings me to the ultimate question: do we stir or shake a martini? I have a simple rule that governs the stirring and shaking of drinks. I shake drinks with fruit juices and sweet ingredients, and I stir drinks with only spirit ingredients. Shaking adds air, sparkle, and froth, and fruity or sweet drinks need effervescence so they are lively on the tongue. All the air spreads the flavors over the tongue and renders the sweet ingredient less cloying. On the other hand, the texture of a martini should be cold, silky, and heavy. So I stir.

But my advice for the best martini is to make the drink the way the guest likes it: stirred or shaken, in and out, dirty or smoky. Whether you're a bartender or an amateur throwing a cocktail party, make the martinis in front of your guests: above all, the drink is a social event, and people want to share in the ceremony as much as in the drinking.

*

67

BARBECUE

BOBBY FLAY

✳

Bobby Flay is the resident chef on CBS's Early Show
and the author of, among other books,
Bobby Flay's Boy Gets Grill: 125 Reasons to Light
Your Fire! *Flay is owner of two New York City
restaurants, Mesa Grill and Bolo.*

GRILLING and barbecuing are two different things. Quite simply, grilling is fast and is used for small cuts of meats, fish, and vegetables; barbecuing is slow. Grilling is relatively easy; barbecuing takes some skill. The first thing you will need for barbecuing is a charcoal grill. You don't need to spend a fortune on your grill, but you should make sure that it comes with a heavy-gauge metal bowl, a tight-fitting lid, sturdy legs, a solid cooking grate, and air vents on both the top and bottom for temperature control. Other features that are nice to have but not necessary: a built-in thermometer, a side table for additional workspace, and a fitting for a rotisserie.

There are several different charcoals that you can purchase: *Lump coal,* sold in irregularly shaped pieces, is preferred by barbecue aficionados. *Natural briquettes* are made from pulverized charwood but held together with natural starches. *Composition briquettes* are the kind most of us grew up watching our parents use; they can be used only if not pretreated with lighter fluid. Lump coal and natural briquettes can be found in home stores and online at barbecue sites.

Purchase a chimney starter, the best piece of equipment ever invented for barbecue. You can purchase them at most home stores, like Home Depot; they are cheap and invaluable. Now, let's barbecue:

1. Begin by filling the chimney with lump charcoal or hardwood charcoal. Stuff the bottom portion of the chimney with newspapers and light the paper with a match. Set the chimney on a flat surface and watch as the fire makes its way up the starter, lighting the coals. After about 10 minutes you have hot coals and you are ready to barbecue.

2. Carefully empty the hot coals into the bowl of the grill and you will have heat for at least 1 hour. This is perfect for small cuts of meat like chicken breasts, steaks, and pork chops. But if you are going for a bigger cut, like a whole turkey or brisket, this won't do. After an hour the heat will go from around 500 degrees to about 200 degrees, so you will need to refill.

3. Keep utensils to a minimum. All you will need to barbecue is a spray bottle filled with water, to keep flare-ups down; a pair of kitchen tongs to turn the meat; a pair of long oven mitts; and a

meat thermometer to check the internal temperature of the meat.

4. Choose your meat: beef, lamb, poultry? Season whatever you intend to cook well with salt and pepper and brush with a neutral oil, such as canola, that won't impart flavor to the meat. Season more than you think necessary because much of the seasoning falls off once it hits the grill. If you enjoy spice rubs, then rub the entire piece of meat with a rub instead. If you are using a barbecue sauce for your meat, don't apply sauce until the last 15 minutes of cooking. Most barbecue sauces contain a large amount of sugar and will burn on the meat if applied too soon.

5. Place the meat over the hottest part of the grill to get a good sear on each side, then move to a cooler spot for long cooking. In about an hour you will need to add more hot charcoal.

6. Place the cover on the grill and sit back and have a few beers. Barbecue takes time, but it is worth the wait.

*

68

BUILD A FIRE

JIM PAXON

✳

*Jim Paxon is a retired firefighter and most recently
served as the lead public information officer during
Arizona's Rodeo-Chediski fire.*

Aнн н, the warmth and fascination of a campfire! Have you
ever noticed how many people will gather around a cold fire ring
during the day, when visiting at a campsite? There is something
about a campfire that not only warms "the shins" but warms the
heart. To be lost in the dancing flames just before bedtime with
the chorus of a pack of coyotes in the distance—isn't that what
camping is about? Building a campfire is relatively easy with
some simple safety steps to remember:

1. Always try to use a previously disturbed piece of ground with
   a rock fire ring (or the provided fire ring in a campground).
2. Make sure your fire ring is well away from any trees or
   overhanging limbs, to prevent starting a fire up in the tree.
3. Carry two 1-foot pieces of redwood to splinter into kindling.

4. Shred some newspaper for a fire starter and build a tepee around the paper with the kindling.
5. Add dry branches and some wood splits to the tepee. No gas or starter fluid is needed.
6. Only one match touched to the newspaper, and the fun begins.
7. Feed the fire with larger dry limbs and split logs as needed to accommodate the number of campers who want to share the warmth and the community gathering. Campfires always go better with songs, stories, and marshmallows.

The most important thing all of us need to be mindful of: when we are leaving, be sure our campfire is dead out! That is where Smokey the Bear's message of "Only You . . . !" is still so appropriate:

1. Take a shovel and a 5-gallon pail of water with you.
2. When the fire has died down to only ashes, put some water on it and stir with the shovel. Go deep to the base of your fire pit and water and stir, water and stir, until all smoke and steam have ceased.
3. Take the back of your hand and gingerly feel for heat. (Use the back of your hand rather than your palm and fingers, to avoid painful burns.) If it is still warm, then water and stir some more. You do not want to be responsible for a forest fire that might destroy precious woods and wildlife habitat, and perhaps even threaten homes. So let us be confident that not only can we build a safe campfire, we can also put one out—cold, dead out.

Be safe, and happy camping!

69

TELL A JOKE

HOWIE MANDEL

*

Howie Mandel is a comedian and actor.

T H E only thing more difficult than telling a good joke is teaching someone how to tell a good joke. To be totally honest, I don't enjoy jokes per se. I find humor based in reality to be much more entertaining. If someone is telling me a funny story that I believe actually happened, it makes me laugh a lot more than something I know is a made-up joke.

Therein lies my theory of good joke telling: if you start a joke by announcing, "Here's a joke," you set up an expectation of funny that you usually can't deliver. Just by virtue of its being a joke, you're putting a lot of pressure on yourself. In fact, some people even exacerbate the situation by announcing, "Here's a really funny joke," or, "Wait till you hear this one," or, "I heard the *greatest joke* today." Now, not only does your audience have the expectation of a joke coming, but the funniest and greatest joke.

In a romantic situation, you would never think of announcing, "I'm about to say something that will really turn you on." You would simply say it, and hope for the best. Then again, if it doesn't work, you can always save face by saying, "It was a joke. Not the funniest or greatest joke, just a joke."

You can never underestimate the element of surprise, plus the added bonus of a safety net. If a joke happens to come out of left field, the surprise can ramp up the laughter tenfold. But, at the same time, if the reaction is nonexistent, you can just explain, "That wasn't a joke . . . I was just trying to turn you on."

I truly believe that great joke tellers make a joke their own by taking an existing joke and somehow incorporating it into their own lives. This can be achieved by telling people that your joke actually happened to a friend, family member, or even yourself. This usually works, unless your story involves a talking duck. Sorry, even I can't help you there.

*

70

BE A GRACIOUS HOST

NAN KEMPNER

*

Nan Kempner is an international representative for
Christie's auction house and the author of RSVP.

ENTERTAINING should bring you pleasure, so it should be easy to be gracious to your guests. Whether your guests are coming over for a meal or a two-week stay, they should be made to feel at home. And no matter how reclusive or shy someone may be—and I am married to a hermit of sorts—I've never met anyone who doesn't love a great party. Above all, on the day of the event, no matter what happens, be relaxed. Be ready a few minutes before your guests arrive so you can greet them and have a drink together. Nothing spoils the mood of a party faster than a frazzled host, or one who doesn't get to come out of the kitchen.

THE GUEST LIST AND INVITATIONS

The first thing to prepare is the guest list. I recommend giving 2 to 3 weeks for responses for a dinner party, up to 2 weeks for a luncheon, and more time for a formal event such as a dinner dance or a wedding, where 2 to 3 months is appropriate. For formal events, send written invitations, but for other events, just call everyone. I don't believe in having a "back-up" list for a party—just invite everyone you like the first time around.

It is great to mix up friends of all ages, and to try to think of people you would like to introduce. It is generally good to have equal numbers of ladies and gents at parties, especially at a sit-down dinner or a smallish event, but for larger affairs, such as a buffet dinner, it's not important.

THE MENU

After you've planned your guest list, you can turn to the details of the party. Spend some time planning the menu. If you wow everyone with a fabulous dessert—especially chocolate—you'll be forgiven for whatever they didn't like during the main course. The key is to serve good food, which often means keeping it *simple*. If you are doing the cooking yourself, stick to something you do really well. Don't try a complicated dish if you're unsure of how it will turn out. Do serve cocktails and hors d'oeuvres, but not in excess, because you don't want to spoil anyone's appetite. The focal point should be the meal, not the snacks.

Informal buffets are my *absolute* favorite. I usually have Sunday-night spaghetti dinners for groups ranging from ten to fifty. Everything is prepared ahead of time and can be placed on the table before people arrive, so you can spend your time with your guests.

DECOR AND SEATING

After planning the menu, think about making your home pretty for your guests. Use your favorite dishes and serving pieces for parties. What's the use of having things you love if you don't use them?

The most fun part of the organizing for me is the seating. I love to figure out who will enjoy whose company. I have started a few romances in my day just by seating the right gent next to the right lady. This is where equal numbers of men and women come in handy. I use monogrammed place cards for formal dinners and for larger lunches. For cozy lunches with family or friends, I forgo the cards and let people seat themselves.

THE UNEXPECTED

Once the party begins, the list of things that can go wrong is endless. People might drop out at the last minute or bring an uninvited someone with them or show up on the wrong day. Others might have to leave early or come very late. Things can also go wrong in the kitchen, or you could run out of booze. Laugh it off. Don't let someone's bad manners or a mistake ruin everyone else's good time.

If you have an extra guest, just stick in another chair; if someone drops out, remove a chair. It's all about having a good time, and about your guests enjoying themselves.

A warm environment, good food, good wine, good friends, and good conversation will keep people coming back to your parties.

71

BE A GOOD HOUSEGUEST

AMY ALKON

*

Amy Alkon, aka the Advice Goddess,
is the author of a nationally syndicated column.

P E O P L E are annoying. All people. Including you, me, and Jennifer Aniston. Like the rest of us, you're loud, messy, demanding, and unsightly, with numerous irritating habits—which degenerate from irritating to excruciating the longer you're around. This makes you a less-than-ideal houseguest. On the bright side, acknowledging the ugly realities of human nature is the key to becoming the kind of houseguest who not only retains hosts as friends but finds him or herself invited back. Now, you just have to heed the following ugly-reality-based guidelines:

LENGTH OF STAY

Stay no more than 3 days. After 3 days, you'll start to seem like a roommate who doesn't kick in for the rent.

COMING AND GOING

Unless your host has exhibited psychic powers in the past, avoid making them guess your arrival and departure. Fax or e-mail them flight or train times, and include your cell phone number in case anything goes awry. Be sure you have their phone numbers, and call immediately if you're delayed.

HAPPY TOGETHER

Your host wants to see you, not experience being conjoined. Bring a book or magazine or take a walk so your host can have time alone. If your host has planned activities for your visit, be a good sport and try to go along with anything that doesn't seem likely to leave you maimed or suffering from permanent hearing loss. If there's something special you're hoping to do, such as shopping, or going for a run, let your host know in advance, so he or she can schedule the nude hang-gliding session accordingly.

SLOB STORIES

Neatness counts. Don't treat the host like your mother and make her pick up after you—especially if she is your mother. (Didn't the lady get enough of that when you were a kid?) Place your baggage out of the way, and avoid scattering your belongings all over the house. Remember, a plastic bag full of toiletries is nobody's idea of chic bathroom decor; nor is an old shaving kit with stains that scream "biohazard." Wash dishes right after you use them, and step in to do the dishes left after a meal— even if the host tells you not to bother. Forget traveling light; instead, travel polite—which means bringing enough clothes and underwear so you won't have to hand-wash stuff while you're there.

CREATURE DISCOMFORTS

Sadly, scientists have yet to find a way to equip children or pets with pause buttons. If you must bring the Wild Kingdom with you, consider offering to stay at a hotel. (What, and give up free lodgings with your host?) Before you look at it that way, add up the valuable fragile objects in your host's environment and compare the cost of replacing them— and the friendship—with the bill for a few nights at the local motel.

GRAFT

Don't come empty-handed. Give your host a small gift—a CD, gourmet coffee or tea, or a new book—even if they insist you "just bring yourself." Treat them to a meal or a movie while you're there. After you depart, mail (don't e-mail) a thank-you note. And if you didn't bring a gift when you came, be sure to send one after you leave.

ROLE REVERSAL

A polite houseguest reciprocates by becoming a host. That said, if the person who just hosted you lives in Paris and you live in Akron, an invitation to be a guest at your place probably isn't the sincerest form of reciprocity.

72

ARRANGE FLOWERS

JIM McCANN

*

Jim McCann is the CEO of 1-800-Flowers
and author of three books, including
A Year Full of Flowers.

M Y first experience with the power of giving flowers goes back to 1966 and my first teenage date with a girl named Margaret. On the advice of my mother, I stopped and picked up a bouquet of mums, carnations, and roses, which cost me a whopping $4 (money I had saved for a Beatles album)! With a death grip on the bouquet, I approached her door. It took me three tries just to ring the bell. When Margaret opened the door and saw the flowers, she broke into one of the biggest smiles in the five boroughs, grabbed me by my jacket, and planted a huge kiss on my cheek. I blushed clear up to my eyebrows.

I love to watch someone's face light up when they receive flowers—especially if it's a surprise. Whether giving flowers as a gift or buying them for your own enjoyment, these tips will help you create and arrange a design that is uniquely your own.

QUALITY COUNTS!

Here are a few tips to make your flowers last longer:

- Give your flowers a fresh cut—at an angle, under water—before arranging them in a vase. Remove any stem leaves that will fall below the water line of the vase.
- Fill a clean, deep vase or your favorite floral container with warm water mixed with floral food (those packets that come with the bouquet work fine).
- Keep the vase in a cool place. Do not place flowers in direct sunlight, or on a radiator or heater.
- Add *warm* water each day, and keep the vase or container full. Every 3 or 4 days, change the water completely and then recut the stems.

ARRANGING

- Place recut stems loosely, but evenly, in the vase. My favorite secret to creating professional-looking arrangements is to use tape to create a grid across the top of the vase, placing a single flower in each of the grid boxes. This keeps the flowers evenly spaced. Add foliage if necessary to conceal the tape.

PERSONALIZE

- Design for the recipient. For the bold, use bright colors. For a "shy violet," try softer tones.
- Who says you have to use a vase? Instead, use your imagination! With floral foam and a plastic liner, use watering cans,

beach pails, or even ceramic holiday containers like a Santa boot to make great floral containers.

- Accent your masterpiece with ribbons or decorated picks— make them yourself or purchase them at your local florist or crafts store. Apples for a special teacher or bells for the anniversary couple will create a special finishing touch.

PRESERVE THE MEMORY

- Many flowers can be preserved by air-drying individually or in small bunches. Remove the leaves from the stems and bunch the flowers loosely. Hang the bunches upside down in a dark, dry, warm room (making sure there is enough air circulating around the bunches). When the stems are dry and rigid (in about 1 to 2 weeks), the flowers are ready to be stored or displayed.

- You can also preserve flowers by weight pressing: (1) Line the pages of a book with wax paper to avoid page damage. (2) Insert flowers (whole buds or just the petals) between the pages of a book. (3) Close the book and place a heavy object on top. In just 2 to 3 weeks, the flowers can be removed.

73

SET A FORMAL TABLE

PEGGY POST

*

Peggy Post is the author of the latest edition of
Emily Post's Etiquette; *the main spokesperson of the*
Emily Post Institute, Inc.; *and a monthly columnist*
for both Good Housekeeping *and* Parents *magazines.*

A BEAUTIFUL table sets the tone for a memorable meal. But even my great-grandmother-in-law, Emily Post, sometimes needed advice on table settings. Not long after her best seller, *Etiquette,* was published in 1922, she found herself unsure of how to answer a reader's question about table settings. Mrs. Post decided to visit Tiffany's famed china department for advice. So where did Tiffany turn to for help? To Mrs. Post's own *Etiquette,,* which the salesclerk pulled out from behind the counter.

THE FORMAL TABLE SETTING

All the parts of a formal table are geometrically spaced: the place settings at equal distances from one another, the utensils balanced on either side of the individual place settings, and the centerpiece in the actual center of the table. A formal place setting is usually comprised of the following:

- *Service plate, also called a charger:* The service plate is the traditional way to ensure that a formal place setting is never left empty. The first course is placed on top of the service plate, which remains in place even when the first course is cleared. The plate containing the entrée is then exchanged for the service plate.
- *Butter plate:* On the left side of the place setting, above the forks.
- *Napkin:* Placed either in the center of the service plate or to the left of (not under) the forks.
- *Salt and pepper:* Positioned to be easily accessible by each diner. If individual sets are available, the pair is at the top of each place setting, either in the center or slightly off to one side. When salt and pepper are shared, there should be at least one set for every four diners.
- *Crystal:* Placed directly above the knives on the right side of the place setting. Arranged according to size, the first glass starting on the left is the water goblet. Next comes the red wine glass, then the white wine glass. Others may be added, such as a champagne flute (placed slightly behind the water goblet and the red wine glass).
- *Place card:* If a place card is used, it is put either on top of the napkin in the middle of the service plate or directly on

the tablecloth at the exact center of the place setting, above the service plate.

- *Salad fork:* Placed directly to the left of the plate, to the right of the entrée fork.
- *Fish fork:* If there is a fish course, the fish fork is on the outside, to the left of the meat (or entrée) fork.
- *Meat (or entrée) fork:* Positioned to the left of the salad fork.
- *Salad knife:* Just to the right of the service plate.
- *Meat knife:* To the right of the salad knife.
- *Butter knife:* Across the top of the butter plate, positioned somewhat diagonally with handle on the right.
- *Soup spoon and / or fruit spoon:* Placed outside the knives.

Each knife is always placed with the cutting edge toward the plate. No more than three of any implement are placed on the table. The utensils are placed in the order in which they are used. If more than three courses are served before dessert, the utensil for the fourth course is brought in with the course; or the salad fork and knife may be omitted and brought in when salad is served. Traditionally, dessert spoons and forks are brought in on the dessert plate just before dessert is served.

LINENS

A damask tablecloth and matching napkins are often used for a formal meal. It is also correct to use an embroidered, linen, or lace tablecloth. The tablecloth for a seated dinner should hang down approximately 18 inches.

CENTERPIECE AND CANDLES

The centerpiece should be in the exact center of the table. Fresh flowers are often included as part of a centerpiece. The options are endless, though the centerpiece should not overwhelm the table. Candles for a formal dinner table are white and unscented; they are lit before people arrive at the table and kept lit until they have left the dining room.

✳

74

UNCORK A WINE BOTTLE

ANDREW FIRESTONE

*

Andrew Firestone is a sales and marketing executive at Firestone Vineyards. He is also known for his starring role on ABC's reality series The Bachelor.

LET'S face it, wine can be intimidating. But my family has been making premium wine for more than 30 years, and I want to let you in on a little secret: the language, rituals, and trappings of wine are overrated. The only real barrier between you and the enjoyment of wine is the cork. Why we stuff a piece of tree bark into a glass bottle is a long and complicated tradition that should have been long since abandoned. At least we have moved beyond goatskins, which predated glass bottles. Contrary to rumors, wine doesn't need to "breathe" through the cork, so a screw cap is really a better seal—and less likely to fail. However, your date is just not going to be impressed if you unscrew anything.

KEEP IT SIMPLE—BUT NOT TOO SIMPLE

The uncorking of a wine bottle should be a swift yet satisfying transaction. For a bundle of money, you can purchase a variety of uncorking contraptions that do the trick with very little effort—but why let technology have all the fun? I prefer the classic "waiter's corkscrew," the little folding device used in most restaurants. It's small, easy, and efficient, yet it also engages you in the process. It contains a foil knife, a "worm" (screw), and a lever—everything you'll need to uncork your wine. You will want to invest in a sturdy, well-made piece, preferably crafted from stainless steel. You can find one at your local wine shop or kitchen store. A cheap corkscrew may work tonight, but it won't be long before all that your worm opens up is a can of worms (in the form of broken cork, chipped glass, etc.).

REMOVE THE FOIL

The foil is the capsule that surrounds the neck of the bottle, and it can be made from a variety of materials, including tin and plastic. It is as useful as the plastic case that holds your new CD. In other words, it does absolutely nothing. Unfold the small foil knife on your corkscrew and position the corkscrew across the base of your fingers, palm down, with the blade facing toward your wrist. Holding the bottle in your other hand, bring the blade to the top of the ridge near the bottle rim. Steady the blade by firmly opposing your thumb against the bottle neck for support. Now simply twist the bottle and blade a couple of times to remove the top of the foil and expose the cork. Wipe down the top of the bottle with a clean cloth napkin or towel to clear away any cork or foil debris. Check to see that while having done this little trick with flair, you haven't left part of your thumb on the bottle top.

INSERT THE WORM

Now, snap the foil knife back into the corkscrew. Unfold the worm and lever. Place the point of the worm in the center of the cork—your approach should be perpendicular to the top plane of the cork, no angles. With confidence, push and twist the worm. This will seat the worm, enabling you to then twist it farther into the cork. Stop one spiral short of the top of the worm. Now comes the fun part . . .

PULL THE CORK

Seat the first notch of the lever onto the bottle rim and slowly lift the body of the corkscrew, steadying the lever with your free hand if necessary. This action will raise the cork from the neck, often concluding with a soft pop. Voilà, an exquisite bouquet fills the air, a perfect prelude to your meal.

In time, the process of uncorking wine will become second nature. As with most things, practice makes perfect—but along the way, the reward is always the same. Salut!

75

TASTE WINE

ANTHONY DIAS BLUE

*

Anthony Dias Blue is the wine and spirits editor for
Bon Appétit *magazine. His* Lifestyle Minute *radio*
segments have won the James Beard Award and are
broadcast daily on KFWB in Los Angeles and WCBS
in New York. He is the author of numerous books,
including The Complete Book of Spirits.

DRINKING WINE and tasting wine are two very different things. While drinking is a social activity you do with friends at restaurants, bars, and parties, tasting requires concentration and complete, undivided attention. Drinking has simple goals attached to it—slaking thirst, nourishment, getting a buzz. Tasting is a complicated intellectual exercise.

If you want to gain any expertise on the subject of wine, you will have to taste before you drink. Tasting allows you to make mental notes about the wine you are trying, thereby adding depth to your personal file of sensory impressions. With each tasting experience you are refining your wine knowledge.

Tasting involves all the senses except hearing (some say that the clinking of glasses adds that one missing element). The tasting procedure utilizes the remaining senses in turn—first sight, then smell, then taste and touch. The following step-by-step technique will allow you to take the measure of a wine.

1. SIGHT

Pour 1 or 2 ounces of the wine into a stemmed glass. Against a white background (usually a tablecloth), tilt the glass at a 45-degree angle. Look at it carefully. Is the wine clear and bright? If it's cloudy, this is a flaw. If a white wine has traces of brown, or a red wine has brickish tones, you may be dealing with a wine that is oxidized or old. The best place to examine these colors is the meniscus, the semicircle at the far edge of the tilted wine.

2. SMELL

Your nose is extremely sensitive and can recognize thousands of individual smells. "Nosing" the wine is a key part of tasting. Take the glass and swirl the wine around the bowl. The right type of glass—one with a deep, rounded bowl at the bottom and a high, chimneylike top—enables you to do this without spillage. To be safe, rather than swirling the glass in the air, place it on the table and make circles the size of a quarter. The purpose of this procedure is to create a greater surface area of wine to intensify the aromas. Now take a deep inhalation from the glass, not just a sniff.

You are looking for pleasant, generous aromas. You want to smell fruit, spice, and oak in proper balance. What you don't want is vinegar, dirtiness, weediness, or stemminess; and certainly not spoilage, especially moldiness.

3. TASTE AND TOUCH

It's time to take the wine into your mouth and taste it. Take an ounce of the wine into your mouth, swish it around, aerate it (draw air into your mouth to intensify the flavors), then swallow. (Most professional tasters, at this point, would spit rather than swallow. This would, however, be rather bad form in a restaurant.)

Look at the expression of fruit, the acidity that gives the wine structure, the nuances of spice, oak, or herbs that give it complexity. Feel the texture, the weight. Look for flaws or elements that are out of balance. Observe the length of time the flavors stay on your palate. Think about what you are tasting. Is this wine ready to drink now, or should it be kept for a year or two? Is it worth the price, and how would you rate it—in comparison to other wines of its type?

Wine tasting is an exacting procedure that will add significantly to your enjoyment and understanding of wine.

76

USE CHOPSTICKS

RICK FEDERICO

*

*Rick Federico is the CEO and chairman of P. F.
Chang's China Bistro, Inc., owning and operating
107 P. F. Chang's China Bistros and
46 Pei Wei Asian Diners.*

THE CHINESE have been using chopsticks for more than 5,000 years. While I haven't been using them quite that long, I have had occasion to use them often over the years. Follow these simple steps and soon you will be using chopsticks with ease:

1. If the chopsticks are attached, pull them apart.
2. Rest the wider end of the lower chopstick in the V of your thumb and forefinger. Support the chopstick with the little finger and the ring finger. Your fingers should curve toward your palm.
3. Hold the upper chopstick between the tips of the index finger and the middle fingers, anchored with your thumb.

4. Make sure the tips of the chopsticks are always even, and the same length. It is impossible to use chopsticks effectively if the tip of one stick protrudes beyond the other.

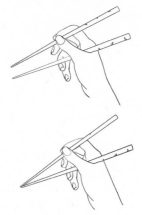

5. When picking up food, the lower chopstick should remain still—only the upper chopstick should pivot, with the thumb as the axis.

If all else fails, you can always make "training" chopsticks:

1. Fold a paper napkin into squares until it is about ¾ inch thick. Put the napkin between the wider ends of the two chopsticks. The napkin acts as a fulcrum or spring to keep the chopsticks open.

2. Secure the napkin between the chopsticks by wrapping a rubber band around them. The tighter the rubber band, the better the chopsticks will work. The tips of the chopsticks you use to pick up food will be open about 2½ inches.

3. Once the chopsticks are secure, hold them between your fingers as described above.

4. Squeeze the chopsticks together to pick up the pieces of food.

77

MAKE A TOAST

CARLEY RONEY

*

Carley Roney is co-founder and editor-in-chief of
TheKnot.com and the author of numerous books,
including The Knot Complete Guide to
Weddings in the Real World.

WHEN you're given the honor of making a toast—whether at a wedding, a retirement party, or a business event—the audience has certain expectations. Listeners expect you to be clear, concise, calm, and charismatic. Here are 8 pointers for giving a great toast:

1. BE BRIEF

Do not consider a toast to be a speech with a beverage in your hand. Whereas a speech can be lengthy and in-depth, a toast should be relatively simple and quick. Keep your words to 2 to 3 minutes, less if there is more than one person toasting.

2. KEEP IT LIGHT

Start your toast with something humorous. The opener doesn't have to be hilarious—no one is expecting you to be David Letterman. But an anecdote about the person, place, or thing you are toasting is a nice way to engage the audience. Try to make the listeners smile—don't worry about making them laugh wholeheartedly.

3. MIND YOUR AUDIENCE

Any jokes or anecdotes should relate to the age and sophistication of the listeners, so know who you are talking to. Don't make "inside jokes" or references that only a few people in the room will understand. It is considered rude to not include the entire group.

4. USE A QUOTE

Sometimes, other people's words make it easier for you to convey your emotions. When choosing a quote, make sure that it has real resonance for you and is relevant to the message or idea you want to share. Settle on words of wisdom that you can deliver with confidence, earnest emotion, and understanding. But remember that quoting is not required. If it feels at all pretentious or phony, skip it.

5. PRACTICE BEFOREHAND

Your toast should feel spontaneous and sincere, but you should have an idea of what you're going to say before you get up in front of the crowd. The key is to practice, but appear unrehearsed. Know the general outline—the opening anecdote, the famous quote, the point you want to make—but don't worry about getting words exactly right. If you feel as though you won't remember the important points when it's showtime, take one 3 × 5 notecard and write single words on it as visual reminders.

6. WATCH YOUR MOUTH

No matter who is in the audience, do not say a single thing that you would not repeat to your mother-in-law's grandmother if she were the only one in the room. This is not the time for anything even slightly raunchy, so keep the toast clean and respectable.

7. MAKE EYE CONTACT

If you're toasting a particular person, turn your body in his or her direction, making frequent eye contact with him or her as you speak. Then scan the entire room, so that the whole audience feels included.

8. RELAX

Before taking the microphone, inhale a few deep breaths and think pleasant thoughts. As you begin, speak slowly and smile.

Remember: the best thing about a toast is the sip you get to take once it's over.

THE BIG
LIFE

78

BREATHE

Bikram Choudhury

✳

Bikram Choudhury is the founder of the worldwide
Bikram Yoga College of India and the author of
Bikram's Beginning Yoga Class.

As **a marriage** between the heart and lungs, breath supplies life to the brain and serves as a bridge connecting body to mind. In order to live a better, longer, and healthier life, you must first enhance your ability to breathe properly.

Most human beings spend their entire lives regularly utilizing only 30 to 40 percent of their lung capacity, with a minimal awareness of breath or idea of how to control it. The first step is to understand how to properly control your lungs to achieve maximum efficiency, which can be realized through the practice of Hatha yoga, a form of yoga that stresses mastery of the physical body. One of the primary components of Hatha yoga is *Pranayama.*

Pran, which means "life force," is described as the energy that permeates and sustains all space and matter and is accessed largely through the breath. *Yama,* meaning "the proper way," combines with *Pran* to define *Pranayama* as how to breathe properly. I regularly employ the following form of Pranayama at the beginning of all my yoga classes as a scientifically proven method to help the lungs purify polluted air, enhance the function of respiration and circulation, and improve overall health.

The primary focus of this breathing exercise is to increase lung capacity through maximum expansion and contraction, which has been proven to enhance the elastic potential of the lung tissue and increase the volume of oxygen in the lungs up to four times more than average subjects engaging in any other form of exercise. Do not be discouraged if you are unable to maintain the full 6-second count during your early attempts—lung capacity will increase with practice. I recommend standing in front of a mirror.

1. Stand with your feet together, pointed directly at the mirror. Interlace your fingers with the palms together, and place the knuckles of the interlaced fingers firmly under your chin. Maintaining contact between the knuckles and the chin throughout the entire breathing exercise, try to keep your elbows as close together as possible while keeping your wrists straight.

2. Keeping your mouth closed, inhale deeply through the throat by way of the nose, filling the lungs from the bottom to the top as if you were filling a cup of water. The inhalation should be slow and

steady for a full count of 6. The resulting pressure should produce a snoring sound in the back of the throat and should not sound like a sniff. During the inhalation, simultaneously raise your elbows up while trying to eventually touch the forearms to the ears.

3. Once the count of 6 has been reached, open your mouth slightly and allow the exhalation to escape by way of the mouth for another count of 6. Simultaneously dropping the head back as far as it goes, and keeping the knuckles touching the chin, fingers inter-laced, and wrists straight, bring your arms, wrists, and elbows forward to meet in front of your chest. At the end of the exhal-ation, which should be complete, your elbows, wrists, arms, and upturned face will rest along the surface of a plane parallel to the ceiling.

4. As you move into the next inhalation, close your mouth and move your arms and head slowly and simultaneously with the 6-count breath until the chin is parallel to the floor and the elbows stretch upward once again. Once you have completed a total of 10 full cycles, lower your arms to your sides and rest for a moment.

Pranayama deep-breathing is an excellent preparation for any physical activity and will supply a strong foundation in the practice of breathing for everyone. Remember: it's never too late, it's never too bad, and you're never too old or too sick to start from scratch once again.

79

STAY WARM

JIM WHITTAKER

* * *

Jim Whittaker was the first American to climb Mount
Everest. He is the author of A Life on the Edge:
Memoirs of Everest and Beyond.

BODY heat is the key ingredient in staying warm—how to create and maintain it during outdoor adventures can make the difference between life and death.

First, you need a fire inside the body (metabolism) burning at around 98°F. Just like a campfire that requires oxygen and wood, your body requires oxygen and food. Without either of these, the campfire goes out—and you die.

On May 1, 1963, I came down off the summit of Mt. Everest without oxygen. I had miscalculated my supply and had to spend the night at 27,500 feet, at camp III. The temperature was −25°F. I huddled in my −30°F sleeping bag, freezing to death. Yet the night before, I was half-naked in the same sleeping bag and cozy warm. The big difference was that I had been breathing on a half-liter flow of oxygen that previous night.

As I lay there waiting for daybreak, my "fire" was dying from lack of oxygen. I could feel the heat leaving my hands, feet, arms, and legs . . . withdrawing into my body. At first light I rushed down to camp II and then into base camp at 17,500 feet, where the air seemed almost thick. I was lucky to lose no body parts and had only minor frostbite.

Lack of food or fuel will put out the fire as well. A friend complained to me that his −30°F sleeping bag did not work. He had just taken it home to Tacoma, where he laid it on his bed, opened a window, and shivered all night. He was very thin, but still . . . ? When pressed, he confided that he did not eat dinner and that breakfast was his main meal.

His fire needed fuel. The sleeping bag only insulates. Like a thermos bottle, it only holds what heat is already in it. Some minor exercise and deep breathing to warm up before you get inside the bag will help protect your body from the weather. Even that small effort is critical to staying warm. Fluctuating air temperatures can be handled by using layers of clothing. Add layers when cold; remove them when hot. Always study the weather and anticipate changes.

We can also learn how to stay warm from other mammals. Whales do it with blubber, but they float . . . and we don't need to carry around the extra weight. However, there are two natural products that are excellent for keeping warm:

1. *Wool:* Yaks, llamas, and sheep roam the world from sea level to 18,000 feet in both hot and cold temperatures—wool is a miracle fiber. Warm when wet, it has a broad comfort range, and the animal is not harmed from its use.

2. *Down:* The other incredible insulator is down clusters, taken from ducks and geese. Birds need to be light to fly, and they travel through rain, sleet, and snow; temperate zones; and the Arctic. And imagine the windchill factor! "Take a tip from the birds . . . go light," my old friend Eddie Bauer (who first brought down jackets to North America) used to say. Down is unmatched by any man-made product for its lightweight loft and comfort range. In wet conditions, you will need to wear a waterproof shell over down. But in dry cold, a garment made from light, downproof fabric is enough; and your down underwear, sweater, or parka will feel like the most comfortable insulation you have ever worn.

So the keys to staying warm are to exercise, eat well, breathe deeply, and layer your clothes. And sometimes in the mountains, in emergencies, with no other heat source, you may have to take off all your wet clothes and jump into a sleeping bag with a warm body.

*

80

HAVE GOOD POSTURE

JENIFER RINGER

*

*Jenifer Ringer is a principal dancer with
the New York City Ballet.*

So you have the perfect outfit, the matching shoes, the coat, and the bag. The hair is coiffed, your smile is impeccable, and you have made it through the day without chipping your expensive manicure or cutting yourself shaving. But with one glance in the mirror, you know something is not right. Rather than see a stunning movie star in the reflection, you behold a frumpy figure gazing insecurely back at you.

Happily, good posture can change all of that. A woman striding confidently into a room with her shoulders back and head held high has the ability to break hearts with the bat of an eyelash. A man standing straight-backed, with just the right tilt to his square chin, will stand out from the rest of the slumped party-goers like a thoroughbred among mules. Good posture is easy to attain and, once accomplished, can draw every envious eye in the room inexorably to you.

The steps to proper posture are simple, and they begin with the stomach. The belly button should be pulled back into the spine—not sucked up into the lungs. The ribs, in turn, should be held lightly under a buoyant chest and shoulders that are back and relaxed. The collarbones should be down, while the chin is slightly lifted, creating a long, swanlike neck. The whole feeling is of being pulled upward from a string attached to the top of your head, with the entire spine stretched and extended. And on top of this beautifully held body there must be at least a hint of a smile, and an assured focus and purpose to the eyes.

If high heels are added into the mix, find shoes in which you can walk with straight-legged poise rather than small, painfully mincing steps. As time wears on, there will be the temptation to allow your back to sway. Do not give in! Keep holding your stomach firmly to support your back, and remember to keep your shoulders placed directly over your hips. High heels are no excuse to allow your posture to slip. If they hurt your feet, then you unfortunately bought the wrong pair. As my mother always told me, "Beauty takes pain."

Good posture can transform you; it can turn you from merely good-looking to radiantly jaw-dropping in an instant. But ladies in stilettos, do not attempt your confident stride on slippery surfaces—unless you would like to display your fabulous posture and swanlike neck while falling down a marble staircase. And men, perhaps you should not dash after your Cinderella; it is hard to look composed while running desperately. You do not want to ruin the effect you worked so hard to achieve.

81

HAVE A GREAT SMILE

JONATHAN LEVINE

*

Dr. Jonathan Levine is founder and CEO of GoSMILE,

a line of on-the-go teeth-whitening products.

He is also the head of a renowned private prosthodontic

practice in New York City and an associate professor

in the Aesthetics Department of NYU.

To GET a terrific, genuine, self-confident smile, it's easy: take good care of your mouth. Many people don't understand that basic at-home care can lead to a star-worthy, self-esteem-building grin.

ELIMINATE PLAQUE

Most important, to keep teeth and gums healthy, control plaque. The first line of defense against plaque is to use a soft-bristle brush positioned at a 45-degree angle to the gums. Brush in an up-and-down motion, and spend at least 2 minutes reaching all areas of the mouth. Flossing is equally important, so don't skip it. To make the process easier, wrap the floss around the pointer fingers of each hand, and create a wrapping arc around the front and back of one tooth at a time. The floss needs to move under the soft tissue in a C-shaped fashion, which wipes away plaque in the critical spaces between the teeth without making the soft tissue sore—or killing your fingers. Do not dig deep into the gums.

GREAT BREATH

No one wants dragon breath. Avoid it with careful oral habits at home. A too-often-forgotten and potentially smelly area is the tongue, especially the back section where bacteria hide out most. A tongue scraper or toothbrush with an antibacterial gel will help cleanse the area. Add this to your daily routine, and you won't be worried about bad breath.

CONTROL THE GRINDING AND CLENCHING FORCES

Because of stress, many people have a tendency to grind or clench their teeth, often without even realizing it, which eliminates beautiful smiles in a matter of months. The telltale signs of this common problem are worn edges and teeth that don't extend past the lip line when your mouth is in a resting position.

WE ARE WHAT WE EAT

Once bacteria (found in plaque) is paired with sugar, tooth decay begins. My advice is to avoid sweets and eat a balanced, healthy diet. Be on the lookout for foods with natural color, such as fruits and vegetables. Also, a high-fiber diet helps remove plaque while giving you energy. Research has shown that unchecked bacteria in the mouth increase the chance of heart disease. Floss or else . . .

NOT ALL STAINS ARE CREATED EQUAL

Thanks to genetics, age, diet, and environmental factors, everyone gets stained teeth. While we cannot control our genetics and age, we can change the type of food and drink we ingest and therefore limit the number of new stains. Minimize discoloration—stay away from cigarettes, cigars, red wine, and coffee. Most of us have imbibed at least a little in the past. Thanks to new products, we can undo some of the damage. New whitening techniques can lighten up your teeth seven to ten shades—the technical difference between yellow and beautifully white teeth.

Troubleshoot problems now to save your smile for your lifetime.

*

82

FLIRT

Susan Rabin

*

Susan Rabin is author of 101 Ways to Flirt:
How to Get More Dates and Meet Your Mate *and*
How to Attract Anyone, Anyplace, Anytime. *She is
the director of the School of Flirting® and president of
Dynamic Communications, Inc.*

I F Y O U want to improve your social skills, romantic life, and friendships, or have better success at your job, flirting is the answer. Flirting is acting amorously without serious intent. Like sand in your hand, squeeze it tightly, and it leaves you; but let it rest, and it stays with you. It is the same with people and is the essence of being a good flirt. Need and desperation are very unattractive, whereas flirting is a charming and honest expression of interest in others.

Flirts are charming, playful, light, fun, friendly. To some, flirting comes naturally; but for many, it is learned. Babies flirt with their coy smiles and peek-a-boo eyes. Flirts have a good sense of humor, are interesting conversationalists and good listeners. They are able to laugh at themselves.

To receive three A's on your flirting report card, improve your:

- *Attitude:* Decide that it is okay and wonderful to flirt.
- *Approach:* Use your body language in a positive way to attract others and look open to others approaching you.
- *Action:* Make a decision to flirt. Practice all the time until it comes naturally.

The three important flirting skills are:

EYE CONTACT

The eyes are the windows to the soul. Think of your partner's face as a triangle, with the widest part at the forehead, tapering down to the chin. Hold eye contact long enough to say, "Hello, I see you"—about 3 to 5 seconds. It is a lingering look that invites a person to return your glance. If you hold eye contact for too long, you are staring, which will drive people away. Yet with playful eyes and a slight tilt of your head, you will have flirting eyes.

SMILE

A smile signals your interest in another person. Practice smiling. Smiles are like greeting cards—all types for different occasions. Take pictures, make videos, ask friends to critique your smile. Be sure it is sincere. Not too broad, like a Cheshire cat, or too tight, where you never show your teeth. Let the smile flood your face up to your eyes so that your whole face lights up.

POSITIVE BODY LANGUAGE

You want to look approachable. Lean forward with relaxed, open posture. Women: Try the lip lick, stroke and flip your hair, fidget with your jewelry, circle your wine glass, play with your heel. Men: Stroke your tie, smooth your lapel, and assume an easy, confident posture. Men and women: Read the signals and be encouraged to approach. No risk, no reward.

TEN TIPS TO BEING A CLASS-A FLIRT

1. Get out of the house. Don't be a couch potato. Watching dating shows and actually having a date are not the same.
2. Take the initiative; other people are shy, too.
3. Nothing terminates encounters faster than sexual comments, canned lines, or threatening conversation. Small talk is important business, and good manners are a turn-on.
4. Learn the QCC's for starting a conversation: ask an open-ended *Question,* make a *Comment,* or give a *Compliment.*
5. To meet interesting people, go to interesting places. Bars don't count.
6. Anyplace can be a meeting place. Make where you are work for you.
7. Have a flirting prop: a best-selling book, a T-shirt with a fun saying, a baseball cap, dog, interesting piece of jewelry. It gives him or her a reason to talk to you.
8. Adopt the three-strike rule: ask her or him out once, twice, but if someone refuses a third time, move on.

9. Don't take rejection personally. Being single is a numbers game, and we don't die from rejection. We just think we will.
10. Flirting is not a one-shot deal. Try and try again.

Happy flirting!

*

83

TIM SULLIVAN

ASK SOMEONE OUT

*

Tim Sullivan is president of Match.com.

MAKING a romantic first move should be 80 percent instinct and 20 percent tactics. The harder the heart pounds, the more doubts that plague your resolve, the more you owe it to yourself to take that chance. Acknowledge attraction. Take a risk and make a move. What we most regret in our lives is seldom our failed efforts. Dating remains a risk-versus-reward activity, a game you must be in to win.

TEN TIPS FOR ASKING SOMEONE OUT

1. *Boldly and decisively declare your intentions.* Don't try to convince the person to say no before you even ask him or her out. Simply and casually express your desire to see the person with a two-part sentence acknowledging attraction in part 1, expressing intent in part 2: "I loved meeting you and would like to see you again." This generates far more success than

something like, "You're probably too busy, and I know I'm asking you really late, but . . . ?"

2. *Get rejected.* If you aren't getting shot down now and then, it means you aren't allowing yourself to take a little romantic risk. Rejection means you're out there actively engaging in dating, and every no gets you a step closer to the yes that will forever change your life.

3. *Enjoy the butterflies-in-the-stomach, slightly nauseating nervousness you feel when asking someone out.*

4. *Avoid pick-up lines and obsessive analysis of the situation at hand.* There is no need to verbally ambush your potential date with over-the-top flattery to justify asking for a date.

5. *Choose honesty over wit.* Save all prospective repartee for the second or third date. When asking someone out for the first time, keep your body language and message open and honest. Always make and keep direct eye contact.

6. *Trust your instincts.* If you feel an intimate physiological connection with that potentially special someone, your gut instinct is trying to tell you that this may be the chance worth taking. Act on it.

7. *Let your fingers do the asking.* An online approach enables you not only to communicate comfortably with your potential love interest but also to express your intentions carefully and specifically. Be genuine and expressive. Remember, you can't rely on your voice, or your sexy smile and confident body language. So flirt, be charming, playful, and sexy, and always spell-check.

8. *Time is of the essence.* While there is no official statute of limitations on asking someone out, it is best to pursue a dating opportunity as soon as possible after making initial contact, ideally within 3 days.

9. *Have a plan for the perfect date.* While the possibility of rejection always looms, anticipate a positive response and be prepared to offer a suggestion that could be easily tailored to your potential date's personality and taste. Stay flexible and receptive to countersuggestions.

10. *Location! Location! Location!* Proposing to meet at a public location—such as a coffee shop, restaurant, or sporting arena—increases your potential date's level of security and encourages a trusting and therefore more relaxed connection. Suggesting a movie may not be a good idea if you've told the person you'd like to "talk and get to know you better."

*

84

KISS

Barbara De Angelis

*

Dr. Barbara De Angelis is the bestselling author of
thirteen books, including What Women Want Men to
Know *and her most recent title,* How Did I Get
Here? Finding Your Way to Hope and Happiness
When Life and Love Take Unexpected Turns.
Dr. De Angelis has hosted her own TV shows on
CBS, CNN, and PBS and wrote and produced the
award-winning infomercial Making Love Work.

KISSING is one of the most intimate sexual acts you can experience. When you place your mouth on the mouth of the person you love, you are sharing the very essence of life—your breath. Your partner's mouth is a doorway into his or her being. In this way, kissing imitates sexual intercourse, and the passionate kiss stands alone as an act in which both lovers are equally open to each other. Kissing can be so romantic, so magical, so sexy, and when it's not done right, so . . . disgusting! There's nothing worse than a partner who is a bad kisser.

Here are some tips on the art of kissing:

1. START SLOWLY AND TENDERLY

Allow your lips to approach your partner's mouth gently, with small, soft kisses—don't just barge right in and plunge your tongue down his or her throat. This is not sexy—it's sloppy! Imagine your lips are quietly saying hello until you feel your partner's lips responding back, opening to receive you. This allows the passion to build.

2. RELAX YOUR MOUTH, BUT NOT TOO MUCH

One of the most important keys to being a great kisser is tongue and lip control. Don't kiss with hard, tense lips, or dart your tongue in and out like a lizard. On the other hand, don't relax so much that you get blubber lips or a tongue that flops around like some enormous, wet slug. Instead, use your lips and tongue to lovingly caress your partner's lips, mouth, and teeth, not to clean them.

3. PRACTICE MOISTURE CONTROL

Some people forget to swallow while they are kissing, and the result is a mouth full of spit. Drooling is definitely not sexy. Monitor the moisture in your mouth and swallow when necessary. And unless your partner seems to like it, don't lick him or her all over the face, ears, and neck as if you were a golden retriever.

4. KEEP YOUR MOUTH AND TEETH CLEAN

No one wants to kiss you and feel like they're eating leftovers of the garlic shrimp you had for dinner. Practice good oral hygiene so that you always feel ready to kiss and be kissed.

5. KISS FOR THE SAKE OF KISSING

The purpose of a kiss is not to get your partner ready for intercourse—it is to experience your intimate connection in the moment. A kiss is not a pit stop on the way to orgasm, but a total communion in itself. Don't kiss to get it over with and move on to the other erogenous zones. Kiss as if you aren't allowed to do more, and make each kiss vibrate with all of your love and passion.

6. FEEL THE LOVE

The best kisses are ones where you let your mouth make love to your partner's mouth. It is the intention behind your kiss that will determine if your mate experiences it as slimy or sublime. If you are connected to the love and affection you feel for your partner, and allow that love to flow from your heart into your lips and tongue, your kiss will transmit that love energy into the mouth of your beloved. He or she will feel that love vibration, and that is the ultimate turn-on.

7. DON'T FORGET TO KISS EVERYWHERE

Kisses wake up our body to our natural sensuality. When you kiss your partner lovingly from head to toe, you penetrate every inch of his or her skin with your love and desire. These light, gentle, unrushed kisses will drive your mate wild with longing and create the perfect mood for true lovemaking!

85

BUY A DIAMOND

RONALD WINSTON

*

Ronald Winston is the CEO and president
of Harry Winston.

A CRYSTALLINE piece of the universe, the hardest substance known, a diamond will provide joy forever. In selecting a diamond, choose a gem that can be passed on from generation to generation and will elicit appreciation for years to come.

THE FOUR CS

In choosing a stone, the parameters known as the four Cs—color, clarity, cut, and carat—are well known. Here is a brief summary:

COLOR

The gold standard of diamond grading is the one created by the Gemological Institute of America. The GIA has created an alphabetical color rating system that starts with D, which along with E and F constitute the finest blue-white to white stones. Slightly off-white color begins with G, H, and I. Yellowish-white color begins at letters J and K and continues to downgrade to strongly off-color.

CLARITY

The clarity grading, or the degree of perfection, works as follows: flawless (F); internally flawless (IF); very, very slightly included (VVS1, VVS2); and very slightly included (VS1, VS2). "Included" refers to an imperfection in the stone, whether it be carbon or crystal. None of the "V" grades has imperfections that are observable with the naked eye. The grading then continues with slightly included or imperfect (SI1, SI2) and noticeably blemished stones (I1, I2). Other details of grading, such as fluorescence and graining, are considered deleterious to the stone's inherent value and require optical equipment and a microscope to view.

CUT

In addition to the above parameters, there are the basic shapes or cuts of diamonds: round (which is the most often considered); square-cut; emerald-cut (an elongated rectangle); pear-shaped; marquise (a double-pointed pear shape); oval; and cushion. The cushion is a rounded-corner shape somewhat reminiscent of a cushion.

CARAT

Carat is the weight of the stone. A carat is ⅕ of a gram.

CHOOSING A JEWELER

Perhaps foremost, I would add a fifth C: your jeweler. Buying a jewel requires a great deal of specialized knowledge received from a trustworthy source. Above all, seek a jeweler of reputation. Your jeweler will be there when you want to appraise your stone or stones, to trade if necessary, or for after-sale service, which might include cleaning, appraising, repairing, or redesigning the jewelry. I do not advise using the services of an auction house unless you are highly experienced. Buying at auction provides no guarantee that the stones are the original ones provided in the piece.

SHAPE, SIZE, AND SETTING

For a ring, choose a shape of diamond that pleases you. The size should fit your budget. Remember, stones need not be perfect. Stones of VVS or VS are perfect to the eye and can provide great enjoyment with a maximum of economy. Two side-stones can provide an enhancement effect at a relatively small incremental cost.

A word about settings: always request a handmade setting if the stone is more than 1.5 carats.

For color, I advise anywhere from D through G. Any color darker than G should not be purchased in any shape other than round because the color tends to concentrate at the points and becomes more noticeable. The girdle of the stone—the maximum circumference—should be fairly thin and even, and the stone should appear bright and have sparks of colored, fiery, prismatic effects called dispersion, which enhance the diamond's beauty.

COLORED DIAMONDS

There has been a growing awareness of fancy colored diamonds, prompted in part by the purchase of a pink diamond by Ben Affleck for Jennifer Lopez. These stones are extremely rare and much more expensive than other stones. Colored diamonds come in every color of the rainbow, ranging from red or natural green to the more common canary or yellow. Their color saturation varies from fancy or fancy-intense to the most exceptional and rare, fancy-vivid, according to the Gemological Institute of America Color Rating. Whereas a GIA certificate for an everyday white diamond is valuable, with fancy colored diamonds it is a necessity.

*

86

PLAN A WEDDING

Darcy Miller

✳

Darcy Miller is the editorial director for Martha Stewart
Weddings. *She oversees all wedding-related content for
Martha Stewart Living Omnimedia, Inc. Darcy also
writes a syndicated weekly newspaper column called
"Weddings." She is the author and illustrator of*
Our Wedding Scrapbook: Memories and Mementos.

TEN TIPS for planning a perfect wedding:

1. BE ORGANIZED

Weddings involve countless layers of details. Keep a timetable of
what has to be done when. Find a good wedding-planning book or
binder that will help you keep everything together in one place.

2. SET A BUDGET AND STICK TO IT

Remember, there is life after the wedding! So set a realistic budget,
and stick to it. You may have to cut back in one area if you want to
spend more in another—if you go over budget on flowers, maybe

you forgo favors. Have all vendors put their costs in writing so that little extras don't end up doubling the fee. Remember that your guests see only what is there; they'll never know—or miss—what you cut.

3. PICK A THEME OR COLOR PALETTE

Choosing a theme helps coordinate all the details and makes your wedding more personal. The theme could be a color palette, a location, a motif, or a specific flower. A wedding at the beach, for example, might have a shell motif on all stationery, and glass cylinders of shells as centerpieces.

4. HIRE THE RIGHT VENDORS

It is up to you to put together the right team of experts to execute your vision. From the florist to the caterer to the band, it is important that you like their natural style. Do not overlook their personalities—any big attitude or lack of enthusiasm will just add stress.

5. TRY DIFFERENT DRESSES

It is not every day that you can be a bride—so look like one. Try on several different dress styles because you may be surprised by what looks best on you. And a note about trends: when making your final dress decisions, ask yourself how you'll feel years from now when you look back at your photos. Better to look classic than dated.

6. FEEL FREE TO BE DIFFERENT

There is no rule that says the dress must be white, the cake must be tiered, and the dinner must be seated. The day should reflect your personalities. A pale-pink gown might suit you best. A lively brunch wedding can be just as elegant as a formal dinner. A big display of cupcakes can be just as beautiful as one cake—and more fun.

7. MAKE THE DAY ABOUT THE TWO OF YOU

Incorporate both of your backgrounds into different aspects of the wedding: the ceremony, music, food, dancing, and attire. Religious, cultural, familial, and regional elements will make the celebration more meaningful.

8. DOCUMENT THE OCCASION

Make sure to meet photographers early on so you can hire the person you love. Do not rule out videography because you think it is intrusive; real professionals are discreet, and you will be happy to have the video later. Make a scrapbook from your engagement to your honeymoon— you'll have so many wonderful memories and you will be glad you have a record of them.

9. ENJOY THE DAY

Designate one person (your wedding planner, a friend, or the hotel manager) to be in charge and make sure he or she has a timeline of the day, as well as the vendors' and attendants' contact numbers. Your job now is to become a bride: get a massage, spend time with out-of-town guests, and enjoy the results of your planning.

10. KEEP IT ALL IN PERSPECTIVE

Do not let the wedding details overshadow this very special time. When the stress gets to you, remember what this is really about: finding the person you love, the one you will spend your life with.

87

CHANGE A DIAPER

BECKI AND KEITH DILLEY

✳

The Dilleys are parents of the world's
most famous sextuplets.

1. Gather your supplies: cloth diaper with pins or Velcro-tabbed cover, or a disposable diaper; some wipes; and a comfortably modest area to change the child.

2. Collect your changing partner aka the child.

3. The child will at times not be a cooperative changing partner and can make the process take much longer and become messier than you had hoped. Distraction is your friend. A cheerful mobile, a special toy available only during changes, or a song to engage your child often deters overly helpful small hands that can make this experience more difficult.

4. Remove soiled diaper and discard along with moistened wipes used to cleanse and freshen the diaper area. Children love warm wipes. Take the time to warm wipes in your hands for a few moments. Some technically enhanced parents have wipe-warmers and swear by them, especially for those late-

night changes when cold wipes have the same effect as a cold shower for both you and the child.

5. A diaper by design is fairly self-explanatory in the description of how it attaches to the infant's body. Make sure the diaper fits snugly without being too tight, and minimize gaps in contact with the skin, especially near the bottom and leg openings. Your laundry hamper and future laps that come in contact with the child over the next couple of hours will thank you.

6. Powders, lotions, and ointments can be applied per personal preference. But remember the old adage of less is definitely more.

7. Tape, Velcro securely, or pin carefully. This can be difficult if there is a wiggling body determined to turn back onto its tummy or sit up and toddle back to playing.

8. Snap, button, zip, or tug up pants. Make sure the child is safe from falling off the changing table.

9. Gather up soiled supplies. Wash hands, and replenish supplies as necessary so there are diapers available for next time.

10. Change that diaper pail before it is overflowing. Balancing the latest smelly contribution in hopes your spouse will break down and change the liner is not only rude but risky. He or she may be able to place that one extra diaper on top and get it to balance and pass this honor back to you. Squishing a load of overflowing used disposable diapers into a flimsy plastic trash bag is one of the lower points of childcare.

11. Congratulate yourself on your success and know you'll improve in the future until it becomes time for potty training . . .

88

HOLD A BABY

BILL SEARS

*

Dr. Bill Sears is the father of eight children as well
as the author of over thirty books on childcare.
He is an associate clinical professor of pediatrics at
the University of California, Irvine, School of
Medicine. Dr. Sears is also a medical and parenting
consultant for BabyTalk *and* Parenting *magazines*
and the pediatrician on Parenting.com.

A F T E R parenting eight children and thirty-two years in pediatric practice, I have held a lot of babies. Here are our favorite holding patterns:

MAKE HOLDING EASIER

Get a sling-type carrier and wear your baby several hours a day. Wear him while you work or shop, or take a walk for two. Because "sling babies" are intimately involved in the world of the wearer, they see what Mother sees, hear what Mother says, and go where Mother goes. Babies learn a lot in the arms of a busy caregiver.

MAKE HOLDING FUN

Carried babies are more content and cry less. Infants and parents can direct the energy they would have wasted on managing fussing into growing and interacting. Dance with your baby while holding your baby and swaying back and forth. Some babies associate motion and holding with sucking, so they like to feed while on the move. I dub this the "dinner dance."

MAKE HOLDING COMFORTING

Carrying calms colicky babies. Here are some time-tested colic carries:

- *The colic curl:* Slide baby's back down your chest and encircle your arms under her bottom. Curl baby facing forward with her head and back resting against your chest. Or, try the reverse colic curl: press the baby's feet up against your chest as you hold her. In this position, you can enjoy eye contact with your baby. Babies not only love to be held with your arms, but their attention also loves to be held by your eyes.

- *The magic mirror:* Hold your baby in the colic curl position in front of a mirror and let her witness her own drama. Place her hand or bare foot against the image on the mirror surface and watch the intrigued baby grow silent. This scene has pulled many of our babies out of crying jags.

- *The arm drape* (call it the "football hold" when Dad does it): Rest baby's head in the crook of your elbow. Drape baby's stomach along your forearm and grasp the diaper area firmly with your hand. Press your wrist against baby's tense tummy. Or, try the reverse arm drape with baby's head in the palm of your hand and the diaper area in the crook of your elbow. For an added touch, pat her back with your other hand.

The next two positions are where Dad can really shine as a baby-holder:

- *The neck nestle:* While walking, dancing, or lying with your baby on your chest, snuggle her head against the front of your neck and drape your chin over baby's head. Then hum or sing a low-pitched melody like "Old Man River" while swaying from side to side. Since babies hear with the vibration of their skull bones in addition to their eardrums, the vibration of the deeper male voice box and jaw against baby's sensitive skull can often lull the tense baby right to sleep.
- *The warm fuzzy:* Dads, lie down and drape baby skin-to-skin over your chest, placing baby's ear over your heart. As baby senses the rhythm of your heartbeat plus the up-and-down motion of your breathing, you'll feel the tense baby relax.

Besides being calming for infants, frequent holding helps parents get bonded to their baby. Holding your baby close to your heart helps your heart get close to your baby.

89

RELOCATE

Cathy Goodwin

*

*Dr. Cathy Goodwin is a relocation expert. She is the
author of* Making the Big Move: How to Transform
Relocation into a Creative Life Transition.

Moving is stressful because your identity is interrupted. You used to be "Dana who adored shopping." Now you're miles away from the nearest mall. Or you're "Max the hiker," now surrounded by concrete. Coping with relocation means managing your identity change.

1. WHO WE ARE IS DEFINED BY WHAT WE DO

Sitting in a favorite coffee shop. Walking the dog along a beach. Raising the best roses on the block. When you move, these options may no longer be available. Therefore, the number one moving question is "Can I still be me?"

People often feel silly worrying about the small stuff—but they shouldn't, because it is the little things that make you feel homesick. The big things—a special school for your child, a cardiologist for your ailing spouse—are never ignored.

2. INVESTIGATING YOUR NEW DESTINATION

Talk to at least six people in the community. Choose residents who resemble you—not real estate agents or chamber of commerce representatives.

3. CHOOSING A NEW HOME

Think temporary. If at all possible, arrange to rent for at least 6 months before committing to buy. By then you'll have referrals for real estate agents and repair services.

4. MAKE NEW FRIENDS

This will take at least 2 years, perhaps longer. The people you meet during your first 3 months tend to drop out of your life by the end of your first year.

5. AVOID LONG-TERM SOCIAL COMMITMENTS
FOR A FULL YEAR

Back to school? Take one course first. Volunteering? Choose one event, not a board or committee.

6. KEEP BUSY

Drill sergeants and camp counselors know: to combat homesickness, keep busy! Create an exercise program. Start a creative project. Explore your new city. Avoid taking action "to meet people." Focus on fun, growth, and self-fulfillment, whether or not you meet anyone along the way.

7. VISITORS

Encourage visits from family and old friends, but don't count on them for a shoulder when you're frustrated. Their lives will go on and, eventually, yours will too.

8. CONSIDER THE SCHOOL YEAR

Move children as close to the beginning of the school year as possible. Don't assume other children will be around during summers. Sometimes entire neighborhoods depart for their "family only" lakeside cottages. Also remember that younger children are more flexible than teenagers. Some midlife adults still retain memories of being uprooted just before senior year.

*

90

HOUSE-TRAIN A PUPPY

ANDREA ARDEN

＊

Andrea Arden owns Andrea Arden Dog Training.
She is the author of four books, including
Dog-Friendly Dog Training, *and is the behavior*
columnist for Dog Fancy *magazine and a contributing*
writer for numerous other dog magazines. Andrea is
the resident professional trainer and field
correspondent for The Pet Department *on* FX.

HOUSE-TRAINING comes down to being a good "doggy time manager." Being able to accurately predict when your pup needs to eliminate means you can make sure he is in the right place (inside on paper or outside on grass or concrete) at the right time. Many repetitions of being rewarded for going in the right spot will develop a strong habit and, in time, a house-trained dog.

Mistakes happen when your puppy is in the wrong place at the right time or in the right place at the wrong time. Matters are made worse when a pup is allowed to make a mistake in the home and then punished for doing so. In this case, he is likely to learn to avoid eliminating in front of you, whether indoors or out.

There are four management tools that will make house-training as easy as possible:

SUPERVISION

Until your puppy is house-trained, keep him on a leash when you spend time with him. If he is by your side on a leash, playing with you or his toys, he can't run loose and make mistakes. This is similar to carefully supervising a two-year-old child. As good house-training habits develop, your pup can spend time off leash in a room with you and eventually have off-leash access to the entire house.

SHORT-TERM CONFINEMENT

To be house-trained, your pup needs to build bladder and bowel muscle control. The best way to do this is with a crate. Most dogs will not soil a properly sized crate (just large enough for your dog to stand, turn around, and lie down in comfortably) if left for a period of time that is reasonable for their age and level of training. After resting in his crate, your pup will need to eliminate, so you have the perfect opportunity to take him to the right spot and reward him for going there.

As a general rule, pups between 8 and 10 weeks old can be in their crate for up to 1 hour; pups 11 to 14 weeks for 1 to 3 hours; pups 15 to 16 weeks for 3 to 4 hours; and pups 17 weeks and older for 4 to 6 hours maximum.

Similar to confining a child to a crib or playpen, the crate is meant to be used until your pup has learned appropriate household manners, at which point he can have access to the entire home.

LONG-TERM CONFINEMENT

When you need to leave your young pup alone for more time than he can reasonably "hold it" in his crate, confine him to a small area (such as a bathroom) where he has everything he needs: a crate to sleep in (with the door open), chewtoys, and an indoor toilet (paper). When he is in this area, he can't make mistakes in the home, and he learns appropriate behaviors: eliminating on paper and chewing toys.

Start by covering the entire floor with paper and decrease the area covered by a small bit every 3 to 4 days. This way, your dog starts off having an all-paper area on which to eliminate and then gradually learns to target a small papered area. By the time your pup is 6 months old, he should be able to rest for 4 to 6 hours in his crate (with the door closed). At this point, you will no longer use the long-term confinement area.

FEEDING AND WATERING SCHEDULE

Unlimited access to food and water means your pup will have to eliminate frequently. Make things even easier on him by limiting his intake of food and water to 2 or 3 feedings a day and 4 or 5 waterings a day.

The more diligently you adhere to using all four of these tools to manage your pup's time, the better chance he has of quickly becoming a successfully house-trained dog.

91

CREATE A FAMILY TREE

TONY BURROUGHS

*

Tony Burroughs teaches genealogy at Chicago State
University and is the best-selling author of Black
Roots: A Beginner's Guide to Tracing
the African American Family Tree.

E VERYONE should create a family tree, for we stand on the shoulders of our ancestors. There are two types of family trees. The first is a Descendant Chart, used to sort out relatives at your family reunion. After all, Uncle Bob might not necessarily be *your* uncle. The second is a Pedigree Chart, used for tracing your family history and listing all of your ancestors going backward.

DESCENDANT CHART

The Descendant Chart starts with the earliest known ancestor, called the progenitor. This person may be your great-grandmother, depending on how far back your family knows its

Descendents of Morris Burroughs

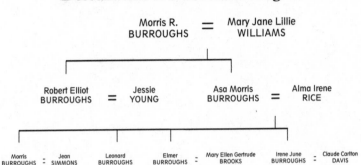

history. The tree will list all of her descendants—basically, the names of her children, grandchildren, and other descendants coming down to today.

There is no standard form for the Descendant Chart because it depends on how many descendants your great-grandmother had. If her son was an only child, for example, it would be shorter than if she had thirteen kids. Draw vertical lines to connect parents to children, horizontal lines to connect siblings, and double lines to connect spouses. (*See diagram.*)

THE PEDIGREE CHART

A pedigreed dog is one whose lineage can be traced. Similarly, your Pedigree Chart traces your bloodline. It starts with you and lists your parents and grandparents and goes as far back as you are able to find information.

Pedigree Chart of Elmer Burroughs

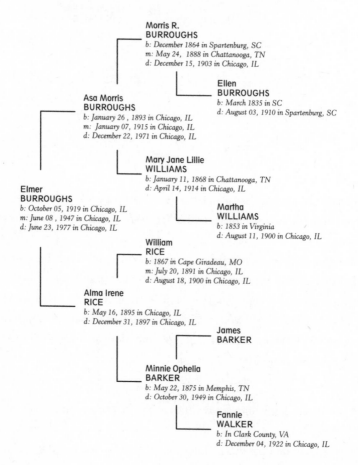

Morris R.
BURROUGHS
b: December 1864 in Spartenburg, SC
m: May 24, 1888 in Chattanooga, TN
d: December 15, 1903 in Chicago, IL

Ellen
BURROUGHS
b: March 1835 in SC
d: August 03, 1910 in Spartenburg, SC

Asa Morris
BURROUGHS
b: January 26 , 1893 in Chicago, IL
m: January 07, 1915 in Chicago, IL
d: December 22, 1971 in Chicago, IL

Mary Jane Lillie
WILLIAMS
b: January 11, 1868 in Chattanooga, TN
d: April 14, 1914 in Chicago, IL

Martha
WILLIAMS
b: 1853 in Virginia
d: August 11, 1900 in Chicago, IL

Elmer
BURROUGHS
b: October 05, 1919 in Chicago, IL
m: June 08 , 1947 in Chicago, IL
d: June 23, 1977 in Chicago, IL

William
RICE
b: 1867 in Cape Giradeau, MO
m: July 20, 1891 in Chicago, IL
d: August 18, 1900 in Chicago, IL

Alma Irene
RICE
b: May 16, 1895 in Chicago, IL
d: December 31, 1897 in Chicago, IL

James
BARKER

Minnie Ophelia
BARKER
b: May 22, 1875 in Memphis, TN
d: October 30, 1949 in Chicago, IL

Fannie
WALKER
b: In Clark County, VA
d: December 04, 1922 in Chicago, IL

The Pedigree Chart looks like a basketball seeding chart. (*See diagram.*) Record your name first (horizontally, on the far left; vertically, in the middle), then your father's name above yours, and your mother's name below. Then proceed similarly with the names of your grandparents.

Next, record their dates and places of birth, marriage, and death. This will add more leaves to your tree. It will also let you know how much you don't know about the family. The Pedigree Chart is used to guide your research.

Last, record where you found the information. Use footnotes to indicate if the source is your memory, a conversation with your mother, pages in the family Bible, a death certificate, or some other record.

There are several places to obtain Pedigree Charts. Some libraries have them, and you can also download charts from a number of websites. Genealogy software programs automatically create Pedigree and Descendant Charts and can aid in research and in tracking your sources.

If you want to take your family tree beyond your own knowledge, start interviewing your relatives and record what they know about the family. Each one can tell you a bit of the story. Your initial objective should be to get the relative's life story. Then record what they remember about their relatives and ancestors. Don't forget to interview your aunts, uncles, and cousins. Remember, they all share your grandparents and great-grandparents. What you don't know or remember, some of them can fill in.

Next, check basements and attics in your home and your relatives' homes for names of ancestors in things like the family Bible, old letters, diaries, insurance papers, discharge certificates, and yearbooks. If you want to go further, search cemetery records, death certificates, birth certificates, census records, and a multitude of other records.

Creating a family tree is easy and fun to do, but be careful—you might get hooked!

*

92

DECORATE A
CHRISTMAS TREE

JOAN STEFFEND

*

Joan Steffend is the host of HGTV's
Decorating Cents.

I F Y O U are reading this, I assume it is somewhere close to the Christmas season (so have a merry one), or you've got a quite a quirky off-season design sense. In any case, decorating a Christmas tree should be a fun project for you and your family. The steps I've outlined here will work for any tree—real or artificial.

Lights come first. You should plan on at least 100 small lights for every foot of tree height. White lights are classic, multicolored lend a more relaxed down-home look, and gold ones are warm and elegant. If you have the patience for it, you can add even more light to your tree by wrapping lights around the trunk before adding them to the branches.

Next, bring out your large ornaments. It's easy to give dimension to a tree by wedging in the large, colored, or reflective orbs closer to the trunk. It's also a way to fill in some of those bare spots on fresh trees.

Now you have a choice to make. If you want a more spare-looking tree with a simple collection of ornaments, now is the time to hang them, either from ribbons or wire ornament hangers. Always hang the heavier ornaments toward the ends of the branches closest to the trunk; save the lighter ornaments for the tips. In describing the "science of Christmas tree decorating," a long-time tree decorator at the White House said, "You just look for the holes and fill 'em in."

If you want a more cohesive "theme" look for your tree, the process is simple. Before you add your ornaments, make a choice as to what is going to give your tree that pulled-together look and tuck or wind any one (but not all!) of these options evenly on the tree:

- Artificial poinsettias
- Wired ribbon: wound as a garland (10 feet per foot of tree height)
- Two kinds of ribbon cut into 1½- to 2-foot lengths: make a pretty inverted V cut on the ends, as though it's flowing out of the tree
- Raffia: as a garland or bows on branches
- Dried hydrangea
- Dried baby's breath
- Pepper berries
- Dried eucalyptus: especially good to add scent to an artificial tree

- Traditional garland: beaded, popcorn, cranberries, paper—
just make sure you have enough to make an impact, draping
it around the whole tree

At this point, add round glass ornaments in a single size and color.
Hang these lightly on the branch and distribute them evenly throughout the tree. Red glass pops against the greenery, and white or gold
gives an elegant look. And if you have a collection of smaller items (say,
teacups or mittens), you could attach them with ribbon or wire. Now
you have created a theme tree, and you can leave it as is or reach for the
boxes of assorted ornaments, collected or made over the years.

I believe the beauty of a Christmas tree comes from the sometimes
messy, homemade ornaments made by toddler fingers. Any way you do
it, it's your tree, and its purpose is to fill your house with joy and reflect
the best of *you* in the holiday season.

*

93

BAKE CHOCOLATE CHIP COOKIES

DEBBI FIELDS

*

Debbi Fields is the founder of Mrs. Fields Cookies and the author of a number of books, including Debbi Fields' Great American Desserts: 100 Mouthwatering Easy-to-Prepare Recipes.

EQUIPMENT

Here's what you need and my favorite tips:

- Love for baking, eating, and sharing cookies.
- High-quality ingredients. Butter is better.
- Light-colored, flat baking sheets with no lip or edge (the lip causes cookies to burn at edges since heat becomes trapped and bakes them unevenly). The light color of the cookie sheet allows for soft and chewy cookies; a dark or black sheet causes cookies to become crispy on the bottom.

- Parchment paper for top of the cookie sheet. It's not necessary, but it reduces cleanup time and eases transferring the cookies because you can slide the paper directly off the hot sheet to the kitchen counter to cool.

- An inexpensive oven thermometer. Most oven-temperature dials are inconsistent or incorrect and can bake at temperatures too high or too low.

- Good oven mitts.

- A long, flat metal spatula to transfer the cookies (plastic spatulas will squish your cookie's edge when you try to transfer it to a cool surface).

- Cookie scoop: I use a Hamilton Beach #40 that can be purchased at a restaurant-supply or cookware store. This scoop will make a cookie approximately 3 inches in diameter.

- Metal or glass bowl.

PROCESS

- Always monitor the accuracy of your oven temperature by monitoring the internal-temperature gauge.

- When placing cookies in the oven, make sure to place the cookie sheets evenly in the oven—that is, one sheet on the center shelf, and the second sheet directly under the first, so the cookies have plenty of area to bake properly.

- If you use a convection oven, you will need to adjust baking time as the cookies will bake faster by 1 or 2 minutes.

- Turn your oven light on so you can check for doneness without opening the oven door.

THE RECIPE

Here's a recipe for about 2 dozen chocolate chip cookies:

INGREDIENTS

2½ cups all-purpose flour

1 teaspoon baking soda

¼ teaspoon salt

1 cup dark brown sugar, firmly packed

½ cup white sugar

1 cup salted butter, softened

2 large eggs

2 teaspoons pure vanilla extract

2 cups (12 ounces) semisweet chocolate chips

DIRECTIONS

1. Preheat the oven to 300°F.

2. In a medium bowl, combine the flour, baking soda, and salt. Mix well with a wire whisk.

3. In the large bowl of an electric mixer, blend the sugars at medium speed. Add the butter and mix to form a grainy paste, scraping down the sides of the bowl. Add the eggs and vanilla, and mix at medium speed until just blended. Do not overmix.

4. Add the flour mixture and chocolate chips, and blend at low speed until fully combined. Do not overmix.

5. Press the scoop into the dough and against the side of the bowl to ensure that the scoop is fully and densely packed. Wipe the excess from the rim and release the cookie ball onto the cookie sheet.

6. Place 12 rounded cookie balls onto an ungreased cookie sheet, 2 inches (about 2 finger widths) apart. Bake 18 to 22 minutes or until golden brown.
7. Check the cookies to ensure that they are baked. The best way is to gently tap on the center of a cookie. If it is firm to the touch and does not sink in, they are done.
8. If they are fully baked, transfer immediately to a cool surface with a spatula and eat, or share to your heart's content.

KEEPING THE COOKIE JAR OF LIFE OVERFLOWING

To make sure you are never empty-handed, take any unbaked scooped cookie balls, place as many as can fit onto a cookie sheet, cover with plastic food wrap, and stuff into the freezer. Once the cookie balls are frozen, gather them up and place into a zip-locked freezer bag and keep them in the freezer.

Making chocolate chip cookies is fast and easy, and you're an instant hero!

*

94

GIVE A GIFT

ROBYN FREEDMAN SPIZMAN

*

Robyn Freedman Spizman is the author of The
GIFTionary: An A–Z Reference Guide for Solving
Your Gift-Giving Dilemmas . . . Forever! *As a*
foremost gifting expert, she has appeared extensively
in the media including CNN and NBC's
Today. *Her popular weekly segment, "Been There,*
Bought That," airs on NBC's Atlanta affiliate
WXIA TV, and a radio show based on her book is
broadcast on STAR 94 in Atlanta, Georgia.

YOUR spouse's birthday is only two days away and you're
completely stumped. Or perhaps you're clueless about what gifts
to give for the holidays. Fear not! Whether you're burned out on
birthday gifts, feeling romantically impaired, or experiencing a
present-finding frenzy, here is everything you need to come up
with that perfect present to wow even the toughest giftee.

The key to gift giving is adding your *presence* to the present and reflecting the recipient's taste. You must consider someone's unique "gift personality" and what he or she really values. Gift giving requires serious research. Remember Sherlock Holmes. Observe your gift recipient and notice the little things. Do a little homework, and consider the following questions and suggestions to perfect your gift-giving IQ. Does he or she . . .

- *Have a favorite color?* Okay. She loves pink. Now, go a step further. Tell her you're tickled pink she loves you, and send her pink sweetheart roses.
- *Have a sweet tooth?* That's easy to find out. Does she love sour, red-hot, chewy, or sugar-free? Box, bag, jar, or wrap up a month's supply!
- *Love a particular author or style of book?* His nightstand tells all. Add a note that says he's a novel dad and what he's taught you.
- *Collect anything?* Elvis paraphernalia, paperweights, sterling silver, antiques? Search for that treasure and tell him you treasure him more, and he's one of a kind.
- *Have any specific hobbies?* Tennis, dancing, fishing—find a gift that fits his focus or reflects his or her interests.
- *Prefer a certain flower?* Find out which one and rename it after her. Proclaim your "own" flower. Re-create your wedding bouquet for your anniversary. Give an elegant orchid if she prefers lasting value.

Next: Remember, it's all about the little things and understanding what makes his or her gift registry tick. Become an expert at the details. Here's how:

1. JUST ASK!

When we were little, we were often asked, "What do you want for your birthday?" When we grow up, we still have that wish list, but few ask. If you want to surprise her, then you can still show her three items weeks in advance and see which one she likes best. Then surprise her with her selection!

2. KEEP A RECORD

Most people forget important present particulars like specific preferences and what they give year to year. Write it down. Throughout the year, write down favorite foods, interests, current clothing sizes, and details that allow you to give the right match.

3. REFLECT THE RECIPIENT'S TASTE, NOT JUST YOURS

It's easy to notice her style of dress, home decor, and other preferences. If she's always in style, then do a little homework on what's popular. There are always trends—hot new colors, accessories in style, and more. Or, give the gift of choice with options like prepaid gift cards that can be used at endless places. Add a note that says, "A shopping spree for you from me!"

4. MANY HAPPY RETURNS

Giving your permission to return a gift is often a gift in itself. For a close friend or family member, you might include the gift receipt in an envelope to be opened in case of a gift "return" emergency. Or, request a gift receipt at the time of purchase. It omits the price but provides the date of purchase and helps the recipient exchange or return the gift without a hassle.

5. DELIVER IT WITH STYLE!

Make the delivery special. Wrap it with pizzazz or include a gift in a gift, like an engraved key ring in a gorgeous purse, or add workout clothes to that gym bag.

Gift giving can be a cinch, but it's up to you to master the art.

*

95

WRAP A PRESENT

WANDA WEN

∗

Wanda Wen is co-founder of Soolip, a collection of
fine paper and stationery stores in Los Angeles.

J U S T follow these guidelines and any gift will look professionally wrapped.

1. Place the gift box on the wrapping paper in the middle widthwise. Loosely "wrap" the length of the wrapping paper around the entire gift box, adding approximately 2 to 3 inches extra. Cut the length of paper.

2. To get a good measurement on the width of paper, place the bottom of the box at the edge of one side of the width of the paper. Bring the opposite edge of the paper up the box's side to its edge. Slightly crease the paper here. Add approximately 1½ inches beyond this crease mark and cut.

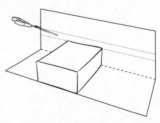

3. Place the gift box in the middle of the paper. Fold in about
   1 inch and crease one edge of the length of the paper. This will
   ensure that the gift has "finished" edges on all sides. Using only
   double-sided tape, place a piece of tape as close to the folded edge

   as possible. Bring up the opposite
   edge around the box and use one
   hand to anchor it down. Now,
   bring up the taped, folded edge
   around the box, making certain
   that the paper is taut against all
   sides of the box. Secure by pressing
   down on the taped edge.

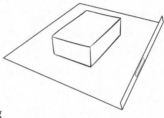

4. With the box in the middle of the paper widthwise, and the
   folded edge appearing on the top of one end of the box, fold down
   and crease the paper against the top edge. Take this fold and
   crease all the way along the box's
   width, to each of the corners.

5. Take both "sides" of the paper, fold
   them in and crease them against the
   box's edge. When making any creases,
   the paper needs to be taut against the
   box so that there is no puffiness in the
   final wrapped package.

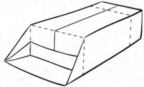

6. The final fold is the "bottom" flap
   that is sitting on your surface. If you
   are working with a cube box, the flap

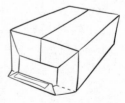

should make a perfect triangle with a clean point. Affix a piece of double-sided tape on each side of the triangle's point and adhere to the box's side. If you are working with a rectangular box, the triangle will have a flat edge, rather than a pointed one. So before you apply double-sided tape, fold in and crease the raw edge by about ½". Then apply double-sided tape to the folded-in edge and adhere to the box's side.

7. Repeat steps 4 through 6 on the opposite end of the box.

8. You should now have a wrapped gift box with no sign of tape. For a purely professional look, take your thumb and index finger and run them along all edges of your box, creasing as you go along. This will create a "sharpness" to your finished package.

9. Ribbon: Estimate and cut an amount of ribbon that will be needed to wrap around both circumferences of the box, including sufficient excess to create a bow. The key is to crisscross the ribbon at the top of the box, where the bow will appear.

10. Tie a bow. Important: do not give in to the temptation to tie a knot first. Simply create loose rabbit-ear loops as close to the ribbons' intersection as possible, cross the loops, and tie a bow. This way the recipient will not need a scissors to open it.

96

SMILE FOR THE CAMERA

KATIE FORD

*

*Katie Ford is CEO of Ford Models, Inc., one of the
world's leading modeling agencies. Ford Models has
managed and represented fashion models for over fifty
years and operates in over 180 countries.*

S MILING for a photograph is the simplest way to create a
terrific photo. When it is heartfelt, everyone has a powerful, com-
pelling, and emotional smile, whether or not they're a supermodel.
The secret, if you can call it that, is to be true and honest. Here is a
smiling how-to with the basics for getting the picture you want.

- *Breathe:* You must start by relaxing your diaphragm and
  taking a deep breath. If you're struggling for air, the image
  will look tight. So many young models stop breathing as
  soon as they are on set. We work with them to help them
  understand that being "tight" restricts a photo and gets in
  the way of a successful image. The same goes for you.
- *Be happy:* Smiling, like laughing, cannot be faked. So if

you're not in the right mindset, if you don't feel it, if you're not open and happy, your picture will look contrived. If you let your mind go and imagine funny moments and light times, your photograph will feel relaxed and genuine.

- *Relax:* your face, your shoulders, and your mind. If the muscles in your face are strained, if you're self-conscious about your teeth, your chin, your nose (or anything else for that matter), you will look it.
- *Trust the photographer:* A photograph is a partnership between a photographer and a subject. You need to be in sync and working together to capture the feeling of the picture. Never work with someone who makes you feel uncomfortable about the kind of picture you are taking or how you are posing.
- *Laugh:* The easiest way to get a great smiling photo is to be laughing when the photo is shot. Listen to music, tell jokes, think of your most embarrassing moments.
- *Move:* A way to put energy into a picture is to move. Try different movements: dance, and be alive.
- *Practice:* Like anything, practicing with different kinds of smiles can help you find a look that you are proud of and comfortable with.

The perfect smile is a reflection of how you feel about yourself. I've worked with and managed many of the world's most beautiful and successful models, and what they understand is that a terrific smile is more about who they are than what they look like. Smiling, laughing, relaxing, and being true are the most important steps to a great photograph.

97

TAKE A PICTURE

DANIEL A. CARP

＊

Daniel A. Carp is chairman and CEO of Eastman
Kodak Company. He was elected to the company's
board of directors in 1997. In 2001,
Mr. Carp received the Photographic and Imaging
Manufacturers Association Leadership Award.

WHETHER you choose film or digital, the basics necessary to capture a great photo remain the same. All it takes is a little know-how and experience.

LOOK YOUR SUBJECT IN THE EYE

When taking a picture of someone, hold the camera at her eye level to unleash the power in her face and smile. That eye-level angle will create a personal feeling that pulls the viewer into the picture.

USE A PLAIN BACKGROUND

Show off your subject. When you look through the viewfinder, force yourself to study the area surrounding your subject.

USE FLASH OUTDOORS

Bright sun can create unattractive facial shadows. Your flash can eliminate them by brightening up people's faces and making them stand out.

GET CLOSE

It is often a good idea to move a step or two closer to your subject before taking the picture. Your goal is to fill the picture area with the subject you are photographing. By getting close, you can reveal interesting details—such as a sprinkle of freckles. But don't get too close—your pictures will be blurry.

MOVE THE SUBJECT FROM THE MIDDLE

Avoid the temptation to put every subject in the center of your viewfinder. Instead, use the area surrounding your subject to bring your picture to life. Caution: be sure to lock the focus if you have an autofocus camera, because most of them will focus on whatever is in the center of the viewfinder! Read on for more about this.

LOCK THE FOCUS

If your subject is not in the center of the picture, you need to "lock the focus" to create a sharp picture. Most autofocus cameras focus on whatever is in the center of the picture. If you don't want a blurred picture, you'll need to first focus with the subject in the middle of the viewfinder and then recompose the picture so the subject is away from the middle. This takes three easy steps:

1. Center the subject and press and hold the shutter button halfway down.

2. Reposition your camera (while still holding the shutter button) so the subject is away from the center.

3. Press the shutter button all the way down to take the picture.

KNOW THE RANGE OF YOUR FLASH

The number one flash mistake is taking pictures beyond the flash's range. For many cameras, the maximum flash range is less than 15 feet—or about 5 steps away. Look in your camera manual to find your camera's flash range. If you can't find it, position yourself so subjects are no farther than 10 feet away.

MIND THE LIGHT

Light affects the appearance of everything you photograph. On your great-grandmother, bright sunlight from the side can enhance wrinkles, but the soft light of a cloudy day can subdue them. Don't like the light on your subject? Then move yourself or your subject.

TAKE SOME VERTICAL PICTURES

Many things look better in a vertical picture—from a lighthouse near a cliff to your four-year-old daughter jumping in a puddle. Make a conscious effort to turn your camera sideways.

BE A PICTURE DIRECTOR

Take control of your picture taking and watch your pictures dramatically improve by offering gentle direction: "Okay, everyone, now move in close and lean toward the camera." We want to keep people smiling, right?

98

LEARN A FOREIGN LANGUAGE

MARK W. HARRIS

*

Mark W. Harris is president and CEO of
Berlitz Languages, Inc., the world's leading
language-services firm, operating more than five
hundred language centers in 60 countries.

1. CONVERSATION IS WHAT LANGUAGE IS FOR

Ninety-nine percent of the utility and the joy of language is for face-to-face exchange of ideas, opinions, and emotions. Learning to speak a language is like learning a sport—it is a skill, not just an accumulation of knowledge and sterile facts. Intellectual intercourse is the most valued driver of language mastery. When you speak a new language, you will feel the excitement of communicating.

2. LANGUAGE IS JUST ONE DIMENSION OF COMMUNICATION

Don't sweat the little stuff. You know a lot about communication that supersedes components of language. Smile, point, gesture, mimic, use the many means you use when speaking in your own language to communicate what you mean. All this will help you get your message across even if your usage is not perfect. The more you practice, the better you will get.

3. YOUR NEW LANGUAGE IS NOT SO DIFFERENT

Look at and understand similarities between your native tongue and the one you wish to learn. If the new language uses the Roman alphabet, you are halfway to learning it. Most languages have parts of speech like subjects, verbs, objects, prepositions, adjectives, and adverbs. Learn the basic order of these words in common statements and questions, and you will be able to guess a lot by deductive reasoning.

4. RECOGNIZE LOAN WORDS AND COGNATES

Loan words are increasingly common in our modern world of mass communication and international travel. Words like *rendezvous, parking, train, beer, coffee, okay, e-mail, amor,* and hundreds of others are understood by urban dwellers around the world, and these words can give you a leap forward with your new language. Cognates, words with common Latin roots—like *ami/amigo/amico, telephone/telefono/téléphone,* and *university/universidad/université*—can also aid understanding of Latin-derived vocabulary, particularly for Romance languages.

5. TALK TO A FRIEND

Make friends with someone who speaks the new language as their mother tongue. (If that person doesn't speak English, so much the better!) Try to find some common interest you can speak passionately about in English. Then try to express your knowledge and enthusiasm in your new language. You can develop a whole new persona in your new language. It's fun.

6. LEARN SOMETHING EVERY DAY

Make a conscious effort to learn new vocabulary every day. Routinize the time when you learn. Tear-off calendars with a "phrase of the day" or "word of the day" text messages are convenient ways to be certain you get your daily dose. Your confidence will grow as you increase your vocabulary in your new language.

7. USE IT OR LOSE IT!

Make opportunities to use your language every day: interpret for a visitor, help someone who looks lost, make friends in your workplace or profession with someone who speaks the language. Once you have become conversant in a language you will never totally forget it, but, like other skills, to be on top of your game you must practice every day and be driven to improve.

8. GO TO THE COUNTRY AND LIVE IT!

Go to a country where your new language is spoken and your motivation and fluency will double. Most people will be flattered when you try to speak their language—you will be perceived as respectful and sensitive. Don't be shy: plow ahead, make mistakes. Your efforts will be rewarded as people and their culture open up to you. Your warm reception will provide exciting insights and experiences that your English-speaking persona would never enjoy.

99

PLAN A TRIP

PETER GREENBERG

*

*Peter Greenberg is the Travel Channel's chief
correspondent and the travel editor for NBC's* Today.
He is also the author of
The Travel Detective.

Ho w do you plan the ideal trip? It's actually quite easy, once you understand that most of us are in denial when it comes to how we really travel. We plan too much, we pack too much, we expect too much, and . . . denial? We conveniently forget our own regular patterns of behavior.

In order to have a great trip, we must come to grips with the concept that it's not the destination, it's the experience.

And when we do travel—even the bold among us who venture overseas—we tend to ignore human nature and our own nature; we really don't change our lifestyle when we change our location. We'd like to, of course. But we don't.

When planning a trip, how many of us will say that we want to go somewhere to do nothing, to vegetate on the beach? How many others will remark that they want to go to a destination where no one will disturb them? And we plan accordingly. It all sounds good, until we arrive and there's nothing to do, and no one bothers us. We last about an hour.

No matter where we go, we still want at least the option of being wired, of being plugged in, of knowing what our favorite sports team did last night, and how our stocks performed. We like to think we're connected at home, and like it or not, we want the same option on the road.

A great trip in my book means that we've acknowledged the above—and dealt with it before we left home:

1. We admit to knowing ourselves and our stimulation threshold. How many hours per day can we hang on the beach before we figuratively take hostages?
2. We need to arrive at a mutually agreeable definition of terms with the travel provider. Ocean view shouldn't mean we need to bring binoculars.
3. Develop a contrarian approach to the time of year you travel: the off-season is a myth. Caribbean in our summer and the South Pacific in their winter mean no lines, better prices, better service.
4. Lower your expectations. Expect to be treated by the travel industry with the indifference you've come to expect from a public utility, and then be pleasantly surprised when that doesn't happen.

In the world of travel, it's not the delivery of the service that often makes the difference between an acceptable and a remarkable journey, but how people recover when the service breaks down. Realize that your first, and perhaps even your third, plan is not going to work.

5. Last but not least, never take a no from someone not empowered to give you a yes in the first place.

*

100

PACK FOR A TRIP

ANNE MCALPIN

*

Anne McAlpin is the author of two books, including Pack
It Up: Traveling Safe and Smart in Today's World, *and
has recently launched a line of travel accessories. Anne
has flown more than a million miles; traveled in over
sixty-five countries; cruised through the Panama Canal
ninety-eight times; and has shared her travel advice as a
guest on* Oprah, The View, *and* CNN.

I F Y O U W A N T to get away from it all, don't take it all with
you. Here are the secrets to get you packing like a pro.

1. CHECKLIST
Check off each item as you pack it.

2. TRAVEL WARDROBE
The one thing most people pack too much of is clothing. The secret
to cutting down on the amount of clothes you pack is to build your
wardrobe using two basic colors. By doing this, the same shoes,

belts, and accessories can be worn with everything. Since shoes are one of the heaviest items in any bag, pack a maximum of three pairs.

3. THE BASICS OF WRINKLE-FREE PACKING

The secret is to pack your bag in two layers. The first layer should be your heaviest items, and the second (top) layer, your clothing.

LAYER #1 (BOTTOM)

Begin with your suitcase open on a flat surface. To maximize space, pack shoes toe-to-heel facing one another with socks stuffed inside them. Place your shoes by the suitcase wheels (this distributes the weight and makes the bag easier to handle). Place belts flat along the perimeter of the bag and any heavy items in the center. Pack squishable items like underwear and socks around the corners and between heavy items.

LAYER #2 (TOP)

Now place a packing board on top of these items. If you don't have one, you can use a placemat. A packing board separates your heavy items from your clothing and gives you a flat surface on which to pack your clothes (thus, no wrinkles).

Begin by folding your pants; place the waistband against the left edge of your suitcase with the bottom half of the pants extending over the opposite edge of the case. Pack the second pair of pants using the same method but beginning from the opposite direction. Leave pant legs outside the suitcase for the time being.

Continue by folding shorts, skirts, and dresses along their natural creases, and use the "interlayering" technique of layering each article (still going right to left alternately) until all your pants, shorts, skirts, and dresses are packed.

Next, button up jackets and long-sleeved shirts and fold the sleeves to the back along their natural creases. Slide a dry-cleaner bag over each one and place them in the suitcase. The collars should be at the top edge of the suitcase; the bottom of these items will extend over the opposite edge of the bag closest to you.

Now, roll up all your knit items (the tighter you roll them, the fewer the wrinkles). Pack them next to one another on top of the layered clothing, leaving the original articles extended over the edges of the bag. When you have utilized every inch of space, bring the pant legs up and over the rolled items inside the case, alternating sides as you go. Then fold up the bottom of the jackets and dress shirts.

The benefit of having the packing board in the center of the bag is that you can lift out the top layer without disturbing it and retrieve or add items to the bottom layer.

SUPER PACKING TIPS

- If you can't wheel or carry your bag with ease, you've packed too much.
- Dry-cleaner bags (plastic) allow items to move freely without getting stuck in a wrinkled position.
- Pack everything possible inside a plastic bag. This keeps items well organized and protected in case anything leaks.
- Organize children's clothing by packing an entire outfit in a large freezer bag. This saves time searching through luggage for individual items.

- Pack women's shoes *inside* men's shoes (if possible), saving valuable packing space.
- Always cover shoes with a shoe bag to avoid getting soil inside your suitcase.
- Compression bags are the solution for the overpacker because you can pack up to three times as much in the same amount of space. Since they seal in odors and moisture, they're great for wet swimsuits, damp workout gear, and laundry.
- Hanging toiletry bags are the answer to organizing your personal-care items when there's limited counter space. Always pack travel-size toiletries to save space.
- Never pack makeup in your toiletry bag, just in case something leaks.
- If you can't live without a hairdryer, call your hotel in advance and ask if they provide them. One less thing to pack if they do!

*

CREDITS

"Sleep" © 2004 by James B. Maas • "Make a Bed" © 2004 by InterContinental Hotels Group • "Do Push-ups and Sit-ups" © 2004 by Kathy Smith • "Jog" © 2004 by Grete Waitz • "Eat Right" © 2004 by Joy Bauer • "Make Eggs" © 2004 by Jean-Georges Vongerichten • "Brew Coffee" © 2004 by Starbucks Coffee Company • "Read a Newspaper" © 2004 by Arthur Sulzberger Jr. • "Wash Your Hair" © 2004 by Frédéric Fekkai • "Care for Your Skin" © 2004 by Sidra Shaukat • "Shave" © 2004 by Myriam Zaoui and Eric Malka • "Apply Lipstick" © 2004 by Bobbi Brown • "Shine Shoes" © 2004 by Sal Iacono • "Tie a Bow Tie" © 2004 by Tucker Carlson • "Tie a Windsor Knot" © 2004 by Thuy Tranthi • "Tie a Scarf" © 2004 by Nicole Miller • "Drive a Stick Shift" © 2004 by Tina Gordon • "Manage Your Time" © 2004 by Stephen R. Covey • "Organize" © 2004 by Julie Morgenstern • "Handle a Job Interview" © 2004 by Tory Johnson • "Ask for a Raise or Promotion" © 2004 by Lee E. Miller • "Give and Receive a Compliment" © 2004 by Mary Mitchell • "Negotiate" © 2004 by Donald Trump • "Shake Hands" © 2004 by Letitia Baldridge • "Make Conversation" © 2004 by Morris L. Reid • "Remember Names" © 2004 by Gary Small • "Read Body Language" © 2004 by Steve Cohen • "Listen" © 2004 by Larry King • "Improve Your Vocabulary" © 2004 by Richard Lederer • "Speed-read" © 2004 by Howard Stephen Berg • "Make an Educated Guess" © 2004 by Stanley H. Kaplan • "Tell a Story" © 2004 by Ira Glass • "Conduct a Background Investigation" © 2004 by Terry Lenzner • "Deliver Bad News" © 2004 by Robert Buckman • "Apologize" © 2004 by Beverly Engel • "Speak in Public" © 2004 by James Wagstaffe • "Balance Your Checkbook" © 2004 by Terry Savage • "Save Money" © 2004 by Suze Orman • "Understand Your Pet" © 2004 by Warren Eckstein • "Care for a Houseplant" © 2004 by Jack Kramer • "Prepare for a Disaster" © 2004 by The American National Red Cross • "Shovel Snow" © 2004 by Anthony M. Masiello • "Remove a Stain" © 2004 by Linda Cobb • "Do Laundry" © 2004 by Heloise Inc. • "Iron a Shirt" © 2004 by Mary Ellen Pinkham • "Sew a Button" © 2004 by Susan Khalje • "Pick Produce" © 2004 by Pete Napolitano • "Buy Fish" © 2004 by Mark Bittman • "Paint a Room" © 2004 by Bob Vila • "Hang a Picture" © 2004 by Barbara Kavovit • "Write a Personal Note" © 2004 by Lansing E. Crane • "Make Tea" © 2004 by Mo Siegel • "Read Aloud" © 2004 by Cory Booker • "Relax" © 2004 by Dean Ornish • "Wash a Car" © 2004 by Charles Oakley • "Change a Tire" © 2004 by Larry McReynolds • "Change Your Oil" © 2004 by Ryan Newman • "Mow a Lawn" © 2004 by David Mellor • "Fly a Flag" © 2004 by Whitney Smith • "Garden" © 2004 by Maureen Gilmer • "Swing a Golf Club" © 2004 by Jim McLean • "Swim" © 2004 by Summer Sanders • "Hit a Tennis Ball" © 2004 by Jennifer Capriati • "Give a Massage" © 2004 by Dot Stein • "Make a Martini" © 2004 by Dale DeGroff • "Barbecue" © 2004 by Bobby Flay • "Build a Fire" © 2004 by Jim Paxon • "Tell a Joke" © 2004 by Howie Mandel • "Be a Gracious Host" © 2004 by Nan Kempner • "Be a Good Houseguest" © 2004 by Amy Alkon • "Arrange Flowers" © 2004 by Jim McCann • "Set a Formal Table" © 2004 by The Emily Post Institute, Inc. • "Uncork a Wine Bottle" © 2004 by Andrew Firestone • "Taste Wine" © 2004 by Anthony Dias Blue • "Use Chopsticks" © 2004 by PF Chang's China Bistro • "Make a Toast" © 2004 by The Knot Inc. • "Breathe" © 2004 by Bikram Choudhury • "Stay Warm" © 2004 by Jim Whittaker • "Have Good Posture" © 2004 by Jenifer Ringer • "Have a Great Smile" © 2004 by Jonathan Levine • "Flirt" © 2004 by Susan Rabin • "Ask Someone Out" © 2004 by Match.com, L.P. • "Kiss" © 2004 by Barbara De Angelis • "Buy a Diamond" © 2004 by Harry Winston Inc. • "Plan a Wedding" © 2004 by Martha Stewart Living Omnimedia • "Change a Diaper" © 2004 by Becki and Keith Dilley • "Hold a Baby" © 2004 by Bill Sears • "Relocate" © 2004 by Cathy Goodwin • "House-train a Puppy" © 2004 by Andrea Arden • "Create a Family Tree" © 2004 by Tony Burroughs • "Decorate a Christmas Tree" © 2004 by Joan Steffend • "Bake Chocolate Chip Cookies" © 2004 by Debbi Fields • "Give a Gift" © 2004 by Robyn Freedman Spizman • "Wrap a Present" © 2004 by Wanda Wen • "Smile for the Camera" © 2004 by Katie Ford • "Take a Picture" © 2004 by Kodak • "Learn a Foreign Language" © 2004 by Berlitz Languages Inc. • "Plan a Trip" © 2004 by Peter Greenberg • "Pack for a Trip" © 2004 by Anne McAlpin

ACKNOWLEDGMENTS

It goes without saying that the creativity and talent of the 100 experts has made this book one-of-a-kind. The experts were chosen based on their accomplishments, talent, and undeniable spark, and I am so grateful to each of them for the effort and creativity they put into their contributions.

There are many others who have also supported me and the creation of this book. My deepest appreciation go to the following people:

My love, Mitch Jacobs, for being the person I dream with.

My dad, for showing me that kindness and success are not mutually exclusive. It is from you that I generate so much of my strength.

My mom, for her unyielding love and unsurpassed cheerleading. From the beginning you convinced me I could be anything I set out to become.

My brother, Tim, for his writing prowess, and along with my sister-in-law, Courtney, for helping me to see through the clutter.

Jennifer Joel for being an expert agent, a dear friend, and the first one to believe in this book.

Katie Karoussos for her unwavering support, unparalleled resourcefulness, and for smiling through it all.

The team at Clarkson Potter: Tammy Blake, Katherine Dietrich, Maggie Hinders, Marysarah Quinn, Lauren Shakely, Adina Steiman, and Campbell Wharton.

And especially Chris Pavone for editing with an expert eye and a biting wit.

My confidantes who cheered me through the book: Paula Pontes (who also doubled as the person who contributed the most categories to the book), Lenore Labi Ades, Niki Assa, Lizzy Biber, Jen Collins, Bethie Ferguson, Amy Fierstein, Michaela Leopold, Gary Lesch, and Devon Pike.

Stefan C. Friedman for being the best one-third-of-the-book unofficial editor anyone could ask for.

The Christmas party crew for their brilliant brainstorming and final category contributions.

And Cathy Ross, a gifted illustrator. We collaborated on our first published work, a book of poems that we sold on the streets of NYC for 25 cents each in the third grade.

My mentors: Larry Kirshbaum, Nancy Koehn, Sally Susman, and Lucy Wohltman. For changing the way I think.

And to my loving grandmothers, Martha Ettus and Mickey Waldman.

And to others who have supported or contributed to the book in a myriad of ways: Missy Bauer, The Bermans of Maui, Lizzy Biber, Ken Brown, John Caplan, Pamela Ettus, Dan Fannon, Jennifer Finer, Jane Friedman, Jonathan Groberg, The Habermans of East End, Kaleil Isaza Tuzman, The Jacobs Family of Mahopac, Tory Johnson, Juda Kallus, Julia Kay, Dave Kobuszewski, Larry Koffler, Jason Levien, Josh Lipschutz, Sonya McPherson, Darcy Miller, Adam Nash, Rob Odell, Peter Olberg, Erica Payne, Manny Robinson, Jordan Rohan, Elizabeth Rosenthal, Robin Freedman Spizman, Jodi Lin Weiner, Jaime Wolf, and Adam Zeidel.

If you have enjoyed reading this book as much as I have enjoyed putting it together, please visit www.theexpertsguideto.com and share with me a skill that you would most like to learn.

Much appreciation, love, and endless learning,

SAMANTHA